D1556876

THE A WORL

SUNY series in Religious Studies

Harold Coward, *editor*

THE ADVAITA WORLDVIEW

God, World, and Humanity

Anantanand Rambachan

RECEIVED
JUL 30 2007
MINNESOTA STATE UNIVERSARY LIBRARY
MANKATO, MN 56002-8419

STATE UNIVERSITY OF NEW YORK PRESS

B
132
.A3
R36
2006

Published by
State University of New York Press
Albany

© 2006 State University of New York

All rights reserved

Printed in the United States of America

No part of this book may be used or reproduced in any manner whatsoever without written permission. No part of this book may be stored in a retrieval system or transmitted in any form or by any means including electronic, electrostatic, magnetic tape, mechanical, photocopying, recording, or otherwise without the prior permission in writing of the publisher.

For informa tion, address
State University of New York Press
194 Washington Avenue, Suite 305, Albany, NY 12210-2384

Production, Laurie Searl
Marketing, Susan M. Petrie

Library of Congress Cataloging-in-Publication Data

Rambachan, Anantanand, 1951–
The Advaita worldview : God, world, and humanity / Anantanand Rambachan.
p. cm. — (SUNY series in religious studies)
Includes bibliographical references and index.
ISBN-13: 978-0-7914-6851-7 (hardcover : alk. paper)
ISBN-13: 978-0-7914-6852-4 (pbk. : alk. paper)
ISBN-10: 0-7914-6851-8 (hardcover : alk. paper)
ISBN-10: 0-7914-6852-6 (pbk. : alk. paper)
1. Advaita. 2. Philosophy, Hindu. I. Title. II. Series.
B132.A3R36 2006
181'.482—dc22 2005029977

10 9 8 7 6 5 4 3 2 1

6431258

matṛdevo bhava

pitṛdevo bhava

ācāryadevo bhava

atithidevo bhava

for my wife, Geeta

and our children

Ashesh, Akshar and Ishanaa

Contents

Abbreviations

AU	Aitareya Upaniṣad
BG	Bhagavadgītā
BU	Bṛhadāraṇyaka Upaniṣad
BS	Brahmasūtra
CU	Chāndogya Upaniṣad
ĪU	Īśa Upaniṣad
KaU	Kaṭha Upaniṣad
KeU	Kena Upaniṣad
MāU	Māṇḍūkya Upaniṣad
MU	Muṇḍaka Upaniṣad
PU	Praśna Upaniṣad
ŚvU	Śvetāśvatara Upaniṣad
TU	Taittirīya Upaniṣad
US	Upadeśasāhasrī

The letters Bh added to the abbreviation of any text (as BSBh) indicate the commentary (*bhāṣya*) of Śaṅkara on the said text. Since the commentaries of Śaṅkara are often lengthy, I have included page numbers for easy location.

Introduction

On the basis of a well-known principle of classification, the indigenous religious systems of India are divided into two broad categories: *āstika* (orthodox) and *nāstika* (heterodox). The criterion of orthodoxy is the acceptance of the Vedas as an authoritative source of knowledge. Among the systems that are regarded as orthodox, the Advaita tradition has perhaps exerted the most widespread influence. Advaita, in the words of Eliot Deutsch, "has been and continues to be, the most widely accepted system of thought among philosophers in India, and it is, we believe, one of the greatest philosophical achievements to be found in the East or in the West."[1] It was also the first to be elaborately interpreted to the Western world. The foremost systematizer and exponent of Advaita is Śaṅkara, who interprets the Vedas, and especially the Upaniṣads, as affirming an ultimate ontological non-duality.[2]

The Advaita tradition has been the principal focus of my scholarly research and publication. In my first study on Advaita, I undertook a refutation of contemporary interpretations of the epistemology of Śaṅkara.[3] Śaṅkara is widely represented in these studies as having accorded only a provisional validity to knowledge gained by inquiry into the words of the Vedas. According to this popular view, Śaṅkara did not see the Vedas as the unique and definitive source for the knowedge of *brahman,* but proposed personal experience (*anubhava*) as superior to the Vedas. The affirmations of the Vedas need to be verified by insight gained through individual experience and, consequently, enjoy only a secondary authority.

In *Accomplishing the Accomplished,* I argue that such interpretations misrepresent Śaṅkara's epistemology in failing to apprehend the meaning that he ascribes to the Vedas as the definitive means of knowing *brahman.* In relation to the knowledge of *brahman,* Śaṅkara saw all other sources as subordinate to the Vedas and supported his view with detailed arguments. I presented Śaṅkara's arguments as centered on three interrelated claims: (1) the Vedas as a logical means of knowledge, (2) the Vedas as an adequate means of knowledge, and (3) the Vedas as a fruitful means of knowledge.

In my second Advaita work, *The Limits of Scripture: Vivekananda's Reinterpretation of the Vedas,* I undertook an exposition and critique of Swami Vivekananda's interpretation of the relationship between scripture and personal experience.[4] Vivekananda is one of the most influential interpreters in the recent history of Hinduism. He champions the argument that the authoritative means of knowledge, in Advaita, is a special experience that reveals, beyond doubt, the truths of the universe and human existence. The teachings of the Vedas, according to Vivekananda, possess only hypothetical or provisional validity and need the verification that personal experience provides. He subordinates the scripture to experience. It is clear that the aforementioned interpretation of Śaṅkara's epistemology is deeply influenced by Vivekananda's formulation and presentation of Advaita.

In *Limits of Scripture,* I challenge the common identification of Vivekananda's interpretations with those of Śaṅkara and discuss significant divergences between both commentators. I assess the consistency and persuasiveness of his arguments, within the Advaita framework, for personal experience as superior to scripture, and offer a historical explanation for the increasing characterization of Advaita as mystical, and the secondary role attributed to scripture.

Some of the reviewers of my books expressed the need for me to construct my own position on the process of attaining liberating knowledge in Advaita. This was a fair challenge. Since my publications on Śaṅkara and Vivekananda were concerned primarily with clarifying and assessing their interpretations, these did not offer the scope for reconstruction. The present work is my attempt to respond to this invitation and to my desire to reconsider central facets of the Advaita worldview. The interpretations of the Advaita tradition that I offer, however, are not limited to explicating the relationship between scripture and personal experience. I extend the discussion to include, among other core issues, matters such as the nature of God, the God-world relationship, and the meaning of liberation.

Theological reconstruction is a process of exegesis and interpretation and there are at least two ways in which this will be evident in my analysis. One of the very important movements in recent Advaita scholarship is the effort to develop a more critical approach to the tradition and to distinguish the exposition of Śaṅkara from later exegetes. For too long, the views of Śaṅkara have been uncritically equated with those of his successors. This task involves the effort both to establish the authentic works of Śaṅkara, and to extricate his interpretations from those advanced by subsequent Advaitins.[5] It will be evident, at various points in my discussion, that I continue this critical process.

Advaita scholarship and reflection, however, cannot limit itself to the clarification and exposition of Śaṅkara's understanding. His interpretations and assumptions must also be subject to the critical process in order for the tradition to be relevant and creative. It is wrong for persons committed to Advaita to assume that Śaṅkara was not susceptible to the historical influences of his time, the presuppositions of his context, and his stage in life as a renunciant. The traditional reverence for Śaṅkara, and the deified position that he occupies in the Advaita lineage, ought not inhibit the kinds of questions that are addressed to his commentarial legacy. His monumental contribution can be gratefully acknowledged and critically appraised within the tradition.

The reader will discern this interpretative process at the many places in this work where I question Śaṅkara's reading of Upaniṣad texts or the inferences that he draws from these. The limits of history and context are evident, not only in the ways in which a particular text is read, but also in the ignored implications of texts and in the selection and overlooking of texts. Limits are also apparent in the issues that engage attention, in the kinds of questions asked, and in those that remain unasked. Let me illustrate this with a few examples. Śaṅkara confined eligibility for Vedic study to male members of the first three castes and approvingly cites traditional sources that prescribe cruel punishment for the violation of this exclusion. This is a matter that has received scant attention from Advaitins, and caste considerations continue to be significant in institutions supposedly founded by or associated with Śaṅkara. What is the significance of caste divisions in a tradition that proclaims the identity and sameness of the self in all beings? Should the Advaita tradition not take the lead in the repudiation of caste and gender inequities?

A part of the explanation for this inattentiveness to the need to reconcile theology and social reality is the failure, in traditional Advaita interpretation, to attribute positive value to the world and to life in the world. While arguing strongly for the origin of the world in *brahman* alone, Śaṅkara does not infer a value to the world from this fact. He speaks often of the world as a product of ignorance and in ways that are not always helpful in distinguishing between ignorance as misunderstanding of the nature of the world and ignorance as cause of the world. While refuting the subjectivism of Buddhist schools, Śaṅkara frequently uses examples that are more appropriate to the subjective idealist viewpoint. The result is a negativization of the world and an emphasis on renunciation. Overused examples, such as those that liken *brahman* to a magician and the world to a magical illusion, while helpful in certain respects, also trivialize creation and imply an intent to deceive. Hierarchical distinctions in *brahman,* such as higher (*parā*) and lower (*aparā*), and the association of the world with the lower *brahman* have the same effect. The negativization of desire and the assumption that desire signifies limitation have problematized *brahman's* role as creator in Advaita and made it more difficult to articulate a purposeful life in the world for the liberated person. All of these are problematic subjects that need to be reexamined and I believe, as will be evident in my discussion, that the Upaniṣads offer alternative ways of constructing the tradition. It is possible to propose an interpretation of the the nature of *brahman,* the *brahman*-world relationship, and the meaning of liberation in Advaita that sees the world as the intentional celebration of *brahman's* fullness, and which understands the meaning of human life in terms of joyful participation through knowledge of *brahman.* The reader will judge whether my interpretations contribute to this end.

Having mentioned the necessity of being attentive to history and context in assessing Śaṅkara's interpretation of the Advaita tradition, it is fair, to my reader, to share something of my own context. This book, like my earlier books on Advaita, is the outcome of my work as a scholar of the tradition. Much more than my first two books, however, this work articulates a personal interpretation and understanding of the tradition. While this understanding is the outcome also of academic inquiry and is indebted to the contribution of numerous scholars, it reflects deeply the years that I spent in the traditional study of Advaita, practicing the disciplines of listening to a teacher expounding the Upaniṣads with the commentary of Śaṅkara (*śravaṇa*), reasoning on the teaching of the texts (*manana*), and appropriating their transformative insights (*nididhyāsana*). Advaita is the tradition through which I interpret the meaning of my life even though, as this work makes clear, I continue to question and critically appraise its historical exposition. My commitment to the tradition conveys itself in the ardor of my discussion, in my contesting of interpretation, and in my conviction that different interpretations matter deeply in determining how life is to be lived. If we utilize Anselm's understanding of theology as "faith seeking understanding," I am not at all hestitant to characterize my essay as theological. Faith (*śraddhā*) has a central place in Advaita, especially if we are willing to admit, with the Upaniṣads, that *brahman* is ultimate mystery. Such theological approaches to Advaita are fewer in number, especially in the Western world, where there are not many persons in the academic world engaging the tradition from personal commitment. In the East, the faith dimension of Advaita is not always readily admitted and there is a preference for characterizing it as philosophical. While there are characteristics of Advaita, as presented in this study, that do not easily situate it in the theological traditions of the West, it is wrong also to deny this character-and to present it as entirely philosophical.

Along with commitment and traditional study, this work also reflects a personal context that is different from those who have been the principal expositors of Advaita. Starting from Śaṅkara, the influential interpreters of the tradition have been primarily members of the renunciant (*sannyāsin*) community who are ritually freed from obligations to family and community. Unlike the renunciant, I am a householder (*gṛhasta*), husband, father, and college teacher. I have obligations to family and community. My inquiry, unlike that of the renunciant, is driven by the urge to understand the relevance of the tradition to my context and the ways in which it can enrich and grant meaning and fulfillment to my many relationships and roles. The center of my concerns and the questions that I ask are different. At the heart of these is whether the Advaita tradition can attractively articulate a purpose for the world and life in it, or whether it lends itself only to the mode of renunciation and world-negation. Is the purpose of life enriched or does it end with the understanding of non-duality?

In expounding his interpretation of the Advaita tradition, Śaṅkara's partners in dialogue were orthodox ritualists (Pūrva Mīmāṁsā), who shared his allegiance to the Vedas but who disputed, among other things, his understanding of the authority of the Upaniṣads and his views on the purpose of Vedic rituals. His partners also included followers of specific schools of Buddhism and Jainism who rejected altogether his claims for the authority of the Vedas, as well as his doctrinal assertions.[6] While these debates have great historical value and help us to understand better Śaṅkara's context, the dialogue partners for contemporary Advaitins have changed. In my case, the circle of dialogue has been extended to include followers of the great traditions of Judaism, Christianity, and Islam. Their challenges to Advaita are different, and my articulation of the tradition has been shaped by the kinds of questions and concerns that they contribute to our conversations. Primary among such concerns are the value of life in the world and the potential of the Advaita tradition to contribute solutions to the major problems that afflict us. I hope that my friends will recognize, in this discussion, some of the fruits of our common dialogical labor.

With this disclosure about commitment and context in mind, my book addresses itself to multiple audiences. While I hope that this work will engage the attention of my colleagues in the academic world, they are not my only focus. I am also writing for the large community of Advaitins, across the world, who share with me an allegiance to the tradition and whose interests are not usually addressed by academics. We must never forget that Advaita is a living tradition that continues to be studied, discussed, and practiced in daily life. Although I expect that many Advaitins will contend my construction of the tradition, I hope that they will all welcome a contemporary effort to articulate and to engage the tradition critically and will see its constructive and enriching possibilities. Advaita has always grown and revitalized itself through vigorous inquiry and fruitful dialogue, and it will gratify me immensely if this work is seen as contributing to that continuing process. Over the past years, I have shared material from my book with students in my religion and philosophy classes at Saint Olaf College and clarified many of my ideas in dialogue with them. This book is also written with such students in mind and structured in a manner that might facilitate use in the classroom. I also keep in view the growing public interest in Asian traditions and seek to make this work accessible to such readers.

My work is divided into seven chapters. Chapter 1 (The Human Problem) outlines the fundamental human predicament as articulated in Advaita. Religion proposes a solution to a human problem, defined differently in the various traditions, and Advaita addresses itself to the person who has come to grasp the deficiencies of *artha* (wealth, power, and fame), and pleasure (*kama*) and has awakened to the necessity for meaning in existence. At the heart of every human quest is a search for *brahman,* the limitless. This existential dissatisfaction, according to Advaita, is a universal human phenomenon and reflection on the limits of finite gains is the beginning of the quest for *brahman.*

Chapter 2 (The Requirements of Discipleship) considers the appropriate mental and emotional conditions that make the inquiry into *brahman* possible and fruitful. The knowledge of *brahman* is unique and inquiry is a demanding process. The tradition has systematized the requirements of discipleship into four interrelated values. A major problem, however, with the orthodox understanding of eligibility is its limitation to male members of the first three castes. I argue for severing the connection between patriarchy, caste, and discipleship and emphasize the universality of Advaita inquiry.

Chapter 3 (The Nature of the *Ātman*) considers the Advaita teaching, proposed as a solution to the human problem, that the seeker is the sought. This is expressed in the famous scriptural dictum, "That Thou Art (*tat tvam asi*)," which affirms the identity of the self (*ātman*) and *brahman.* This identity is explained by questioning conventional understanding of the nature of the self as non-different from body, senses, and mind and elucidating its nature as awareness, timeless, all-pervasive, bliss, and non-dual. Traditional methods, employed by Advaita teachers, for pointing to the self as unlimited, nonobjective awareness are also discussed.

Chapter 4 (The Source of Valid Knowledge) considers the source of the Advaita teaching about the nature of reality. Advaita does not deny the experiential character of the self. It is because of the self that one has an indubitable sense of existence and the experience of bliss (*ānanda*).[7] The experience of the self as existence and bliss is not the same as knowledge. The role of the scripture in relation to the experience of *brahman* as existence and bliss is to correct misunderstanding and to identify these with the nature of *brahman.* Knowledge also gives rise to a mental and emotional disposition that reflects and is consistent with proper understanding of the self. This chapter also examines the unique method through which *brahman,* unavailable for any form of objectification, is known through the words of the Upaniṣads. Even so, the intrinsic nature of *brahman* can never revealed as it transcends all comprehension and definition.

Chapter 5 (*Brahman* as the World) turns to a consideration of the significance of the world in relation to *brahman.* If *brahman* is non-dual and limitless, how are we to understand the status of the world? Some Advaita commentators appear to suggest that the knowledge of *brahman* results in the eradication of all diversity and deny any reality to the world. In this chapter, I question such interpretations of the *brahman*-world relationship. It is not at all necessary to to deny the reality and value of the world in order to affirm the non-dual and limitless nature of *brahman.* To understand the world as an effect and as ontologically non-different from *brahman* does not require us to grant the same value to the world as we do to *brahman,* but it does not require us also to deny or negate the world. The world may be understood to be a celebrative expression of *brahman's* fullness. Its value lies in the fact that it partakes of the nature of *brahman,* even though, as a finite entity, it can never fully express *brahman.*

Chapter 6 (*Brahman* as God) focuses on the issue of hierarchies in *brahman.* Advaita interpreters generally distinguish between two orders of *brahman* and suggest a hierarchy between these. One is *parā,* or higher, *brahman* and the other is *aparā*, or lower, *brahman.* The higher *brahman* is presented as the absolute, non-dual reality, transcending space, time, and causal relations. It cannot be the source of the world, since it is considered to be beyond causation and activity. The cause of the world is the lower *brahman,* usually identified with God *(īśvara).* I query the necessity for such distinctions in *brahman* and argue that the need for bifurcation in the nature of *brahman* is obviated if *brahman's* relationship with the world is not thought of as implying any limits or loss of nature. This is, in fact, suggested in the Upaniṣads. It is not also necessary to deny purpose in *brahman,* if such purpose is not equated with the limitations of desire in a finite being, subject to ignorance.

Chapter 7 (Liberation) outlines and clarifies the multiple implications of liberation in Advaita. Although the tradition has emphasized ignorance (*avidyā*) as the root cause of suffering, Advaitins should not ignore the suffering that human beings experience in conditions of want and through oppression based on gender and caste. There is a need to consider the broader implications of *mokṣa* for social, political, and economic relationships and to account for human suffering, broadly construed. While the Advaita tradition has had a very limited understanding of the role of the liberated, there is nothing inherent in the nature of liberation that makes actions for the well-being of others impossible. On the contrary, the understanding of self that is synonymous with the attainment of liberation, provides a powerful impetus for a life of service and compassion. The kinds of activity that are possible for a liberated person do not have to be narrowly construed, but the tradition must articulate a positive value for the world and engagement within it. Liberation does not have to be interpreted in ways that seem to bring purposeful living to an end.

I want to express my gratitude to Saint Olaf College for granting me leave from my teaching responsibilities to complete this work. I am also grateful for the unfailing support of my wife, Geeta, and our children, Ishanaa, Akshar, and Ashesh. The reviewers for the State University of New York Press offered helpful suggestions and I have also benefited from the criticism of my Advaitin friends, Narayanan Ramasamy and Martha Doherty. My editors at the State University of New York Press efficiently guided and supported me through the publication process. I am indebted to Harold Coward, editor of Series in Religious Studies, for his confidence in my work. My mother passed away suddenly before this book could be published. My education is her gift and she would be full of happiness and pride.

CHAPTER ONE

The Human Problem

The Chāndogya Upaniṣad describes an encounter between a student named Nārada and his teacher, Sanatkumāra.[1] Nārada desired religious instruction from Sanatkumāra, but the teacher requested him to describe first the various intellectual disciplines and skills that he had already acquired and mastered. Nārada went on to provide an exhaustive list that included the four Vedas, the Mahābhārata, grammar, rituals, mathematics, logic, ethics, philology, war, physical science, astronomy, and the fine arts! At the end of it all, he confessed to his teacher that, in spite of all the knowledge he had mastered, he was in sorrow and requested his teacher's help in overcoming his sorrow.

In the Bṛhadāraṇyaka Upaniṣad, we encounter the famous teacher Yājñavalkya and his wives, Maitreyī and Kātyāyanī.[2] Yājñavalkya informs his wives that he is ready to enter the order of monasticism or the fourth stage of a traditionally ordered Hindu life.[3] Before doing so, he wants to distribute his wealth between both of them. The Upaniṣad records the ensuing conversation betweeen Yājñavalkya and his wife, Maitreyī.

> "Maitreyī, I am about to go away from this place. So come, let me make a settlement between you and Kātyāyanī."
>
> Maitreyī asked in reply: "If I were to possess the entire world filled with wealth, sir, would it make me immortal?" "No," said Yājñavalkya, "it will only permit you to live the life of a wealthy person. Through wealth one cannot expect immortality."
>
> "What is the point in getting something that will not make me immortal?" retorted Maitreyī. "Tell me instead, sir, all that you know."

These two dialogues are typical of encounters between seekers and teachers (*gurus*) in the Upaniṣads and illustrate central aspects of the Advaita understanding of the fundamental human predicament.

THE LIMITS OF KNOWLEDGE

In the case of Nārada, the Upaniṣad obviously wants to comment on the limitations of secular knowledge and scriptural learning that do not address and resolve the fundamental problem of human sorrow. In the Muṇḍaka Upaniṣad the teacher, Aṅgiras, distinguishes between two kinds of knowledge and refers to these as higher knowledge (*parā vidyā*) and lower knowledge (*aparā vidyā*).[4] Included in the category of lower knowledge are the four Vedas (Ṛg, Sāma, Yajur, and Atharva), phonetics, ritual, grammar, etymology, metrics, and astronomy. The authoritative scriptures are included here, not to devalue their significance, but to distinguish between a superficial mastery and memorization of the words of the texts and the deeper liberating wisdom that is the result when a mature seeker, with the aid of a teacher, approaches the texts.[5] Higher knowledge, on the other hand, is described as that by which one attains the imperishable.[6] Through it, the wise come to know "What cannot be seen, what cannot be grasped, without colour, without sight or hearing, without hands or feet; What is eternal and and all-pervading, extremely minute, present everywhere—That is the immutable, which the wise fully perceive."[7]

A well-known story explaining the circumstances leading to the composition of a famous poetic text, the *Bhajagovindam,* tells of an incident involving Śaṅkara and his disciples in the holy city of Varanasi. One day, while on his customary walk, Śaṅkara heard, amidst the general din and chaos of the city, the sounds of someone trying to memorize a grammar rule by repetition. The famous teacher's curiosity was aroused and, as he approached the source of the sound, he encountered an unusual sight. Before him sat an old, toothless man, with sparkling white hair, wrinkled skin, and a bent back. In his hand, was an equally aged Sanskrit grammar text held close to his eyes. The old man was absorbed in laboring to memorize a rule of grammar. While not condemning the old man's persistence, Śaṅkara used the occasion to remind him of the limits of grammatical knowledge in the first verse of the poem. This verse is also sung as a refrain throughout the text.

> Adore the Lord, adore the Lord, adore the Lord, O fool! When the appointed time (for departure) comes, the repetition of grammatical rules will not, indeed, save you.[8]

Advaita and, broadly speaking, the Hindu tradition, it must be emphasized, does not condemn the pursuit of secular knowledge, or *aparā vidyā.* The spectacular achievements of human civilization are directly attributable to discoveries and breakthroughs in this field. The criticism leveled against *aparā vidyā* is very specific. Such knowledge does not liberate one from the anxiety and fear of mortality or satisfy the human urge for fullness of being. Its field is the realm of the finite and perishable and it does not, as the Muṇḍaka Upaniṣad reminds us, lead to the imperishable. In spite of all the accomplishments of technology and our mastery of the universe, secular knowledge, as

Nārada discovered, still leaves the human being with a deep and inexplicable sorrow, a sense of inner lack and incompleteness. Nārada's need for a deeper meaning to his existence could not be satisfied by information about the world gained through the numerous intellectual disciplines that he enumerated.

THE LIMITS OF WEALTH

If Nārada's longing for the ultimate was awakened by his experience of the limits of secular knowledge, Maitreyī awoke to her need for the eternal through her understanding of the limitations of materialism. She does not ask her husband, Yājñavalkya, if wealth has any value. Her question is quite specific. She wants to know whether she could attain immortality through wealth and his answer, as we have noted, is negative.

The Hindu tradition, on the whole, is not antimaterialistic or averse to wealth.[9] *Artha* (wealth) is one of the four legitimate goals of Hindu life along with pleasure (*kāma*), virtue (*dharma*), and liberation (*mokṣa*). In the *Rāmacaritamānasa,* a sixteenth-century Hindi vernacular poetic reworking of the story of Rama, by Tulasīdāsa, a disciple asks his teacher, "What is the greatest human suffering?" "There is no suffering in the world as great as poverty," replies his teacher without hesitation.[10] The tradition has never glorified involuntary poverty. A utopian society, as envisaged by the poet Tulasīdāsa, is one that is free from suffering occasioned by poverty.

> There was no premature death or suffering of any kind; everyone enjoyed beauty and health. No one was poor, sorrowful or in want; no one was ignorant or devoid of auspicious marks.[11]

While the significance of wealth and its role in human well-being are recognized, there are specific guidelines for its acquisition and use. In the popular schematization of the four goals of life, *dharma,* which includes ethics and moral values, serves to regulate the pursuit of wealth (*artha*) and pleasure (*kāma*). *Dharma* emphasizes the social and interconnected character of existence and requires us to be cognizant of the effects, positive and negative, of wealth-producing activities. It is a violation of *dharma,* for example, to accumulate wealth through methods that inflict suffering on others, that are unjust, and that deplete the resources of the community. A person who selfishly exploits the resources of the community to gain wealth, without care for its well-being and without striving to replenish these resources, is described and condemned in the Bhagavadgītā as a thief. Such a person enjoys the gifts of the community and nature without giving anything in return.[12]

Wealth is not an end in itself. It must be acquired by legitimate means and used to satisfy personal and family needs. It ought to be shared also with those who are in want. *Dāna*, or generosity, is a core value and a central teaching.[13] There are specific guidelines provided in the tradition for sharing and distributing wealth. First, generosity should be motivated by the conviction that it is good and noble to share. The suggestion here is that we should not give with the expectation of receiving a favor from the recipient or with the motive of attracting the attention and praise of others. Second, it is need that should dictate our choice of a recipient and not considerations such as religion, ethnicity, or nationality. Third, our generosity must be quick and timely. Fourth, our gifts must be shared with the needy in the right places. The choice of an appropriate place to distribute our gifts should be influenced by our concern for accessibility and the dignity and self-respect of the receiver. Places and times should not be selected with the intention of enhancing the public reputation of the donor.

While generosity is encouraged and wealth not condemned, the same cannot be said for greed. The tradition speaks eloquently and continuously about the problems and dangers of greed. Greed is regarded as a direct cause of evil action and suffering and as a force that impels human beings, even unwillingly, to do wrong. One who is able to resist its impulse is considered to be disciplined and happy.[14] Although it is true that there are some human beings who are quite content with wealth in moderation, there are many others who are perpetually discontented in spite of abundance. They are driven by an immoderate, and what seems to them to be a natural, urge for wealth. They become victims of a greed that can never be quenched. Greed and peace, in the perspective of the tradition, are incompatible because greed is a condition of discontent that keeps one feeling that one never has enough. Greed is an obsession about acquisition. The Bhagavadgītā presents a detailed psychological profile of this obsession, capturing the anxiety, arrogance, self-centeredness, and competitiveness that are its essential ingredients.

> This has been obtained by me today;
> This wish I shall attain;
> This is, and this wealth also,
> Shall be mine.
> That enemy has been slain my me,
> And I shall slay others too;
> I am the Lord, I am the enjoyer,
> I am successful, powerful and happy.[15]

A human being is likely to become a victim of greed when wealth becomes the central means of achieving self-value and meaning. There is an increasing likelihood of this in a community where consumerism and materialistic success are glorified. The problem, however, is that the value that one may confer on oneself as a consequence of possessions is not an independent or absolute one. The meaning and worth of one's wealth is relative to the material worth of others and self-value turns out to be a fluctuating commodity. Self-worth increases when one's assets are worth more than one's rivals' and is diminished when these assets decline in value. The consequence is a state of anxiety and insecurity fed by a constant evaluation of oneself in relation to others and the perception of others as rivals and threats to one's sense of self-adequacy. One is now a participant in a race without a finishing line and without any hope of attaining contentment. A more accurate analogy is a race with a distant finishing line that recedes each time one approaches it.

The greed for wealth reduces the value of the human being to a quantifiable economic quantity. The question, "What is his worth?" is one that sharply expresses this outlook since it equates the value of a person with his or her material assets. The significance of the person is not distinguished from possessions, but fully identified with the economic quantification of these. The greed for wealth is likened to a voracious fire that will not be satiated, but only increases in intensity with the fuel of acquisition. There is also, as Maitreyī understood, a finite quality to all material things which adds to their ultimately unsatisfactory character.

What is true of wealth is also, as Huston Smith reminds us, true of gains such as power and fame. When these become the principal focus of our quest for meaning and value, we condemn ourselves to anxiety and uncertainty. "The idea of a nation," Smith writes, "in which everyone is famous is a contradiction in terms; and if power were distributed equally, no one would be powerful in the sense in which we customarily use the word. From the competitiveness of these goods to their precariousness is a short step. As other people want them too, who knows when success will change hands?"[16]

THE LIMITS OF PLEASURE

The Kaṭha Upaniṣad begins with the story of Uśan, son of Vājaśravā, who is performing a religious ritual in which he is expected to give all his possessions away. His son, Naciketas, however, observes that his father is contravening the requirements of the ritual by giving away only those cows that are old and incapable of producing young. To dramatically draw his father's attention to this flaw, Naciketas says, "Father, to whom will you give me?" Surprised by his son's question, Uśan does not reply and Naciketas repeats his question three times. Eventually, in a fit of anger, Uśan shouts, "I'll give you to Death!"

Naciketas reaches the abode of Yama, lord of death, but discovers that Yama is not there. He patiently awaits his return for three days and nights without food and water. Yama is very apologetic when he returns and offers Naciketas three boons as a form of compensation. For his first boon, Naciketas requests that his father be free from anxiety and from anger toward him. For his second boon, he asks for the details of a fire ritual for the attainment of the heavenly world. Yama readily grants his desires.

The boy's third request surprises Yama. "There is this doubt about a man who is dead. 'He exists,' says some; others, 'He exists not.' I want to know this so please teach me. This is the third of my three wishes."[17] Yama pleads to be relieved of the difficulty of teaching about this subject because of its subtlety and difficulty of comprehension. "Choose sons and grandsons who'd live a hundred years! Plenty of livestock and elephants, horses and gold! Choose as your domain a wide expanse of of earth! And you yourself live as many autumns as you wish!" Yama offers him a long life, wealth, prominence in the world, and sexual pleasures. Naciketas turns down the generous offer of Yama with a powerful statement on the limits of wealth and the pleasures that it affords.

> Since the passing days of a mortal, O death,
> sap here the energy of all the senses;
> And even a full life is but a trifle;
> so keep your horses, your songs and dances!
>
> With wealth, you cannot make a man content;
> Will we get to keep wealth, when we have seen you?
> And we get to live only as long as you will allow!
> So this alone is the wish that I'd like to choose.[18]

The youth's observation to Yama that the human being will never be content with wealth alone is at the heart of the tradition's indictment of pleasure and materialism. Materialism lures us with a dazzling but false promise of contentment. We are induced to expend our energies in a vain quest that leaves us with a feeling of inadequacy and emptiness. "The spiritual problem with greed," as David Loy observes, "—both the greed for profit and the greed to consume—is due not only to the consequent maldistribution of worldly goods (although a more equitable distribution is, of course, essential), or to its effects on the biosphere, but even more fundamentally because greed is based on a delusion: the delusion that happiness is to be found this way."[19]

Naciketas comments also on the transient character of worldly pleasures, a common theme in Hindu sacred texts. In clarifying this critique, however, it must be stated that the Hindu tradition is not opposed to pleasurable experiences in the world. *Kāma* (pleasure) is one of the four approved goals to which we have already referred. As with the quest for wealth, there are guidelines within which pleasure may be legitimately sought. One ought not to pursue pleasure through methods that are injurious to self or that exploit and cause suffering to others. In the search for pleasure, one must follow basic moral values (*dharma*) and be considerate to others. In the Bhagavadgītā (7:11), Kṛṣṇa gives his approval to pleasure by stating, "I am pleasure which is not opposed to righteousness."[20]

While approving of pleasures within the ambit of *dharma,* the text cautions that unnecessary frustration and pain can be avoided if we understand the limitations of sense pleasures. Kṛṣṇa offers a pertinent and succinct comment in this regard.

> Pleasures born out of contact, indeed,
> Are wombs (i.e. sources) of pain,
> Since they have a beginning and an end (i.e. are not eternal), Son of Kuntī,
> The wise person is not content in them.[21]

Kṛṣṇa does not deny the pleasures of sensual experiences, but realistically identifies their central limitation. By describing these as having a beginning and an end, he is pointing, like Naciketas, to their transient character. The temporary quality of sense-enjoyments is a consequence of the unstable nature of the factors that make such experiences possible. The sense-object is subject to time and change, the relevant sense organ is gradually worn out through indulgence, and the mind grows saturated and bored with repetitiveness.

The human being who is addicted to sense gratification of any kind is caught in a vicious circle. He is in search of an enduring happiness but does so through fleeting and impermanent experiences. Although dissatisfied, he turns again and again to these momentary forms of pleasure and, before long, becomes hopelessly addicted and dependent. The problem is not in the nature of the sense experience, but in unrealistic expectations of what we may gain from it. When we understand that lasting joy is not to be found through temporary sense experiences we take a significant step toward maturity and wisdom.

THE REFLECTIVE LIFE

The Advaita tradition claims that if we live our lives thoughtfully and reflect, with detachment, on our experiences, each of us will come to experience, like Nārada, Maitreyī, and Naciketas, that the achievement of wealth, power, fame, and pleasure leave us unfulfilled. This awakening may be sudden or gradual and is not to be equated with chronological aging. The young Naciketas of the Kaṭha Upaniṣad came to this realization, while the old man, on the brink of death in the *Bhajagovindam,* did not. It depends entirely on how we exercise our human capacity for self-critical reflection.

It must be emphasized that this moment of awakening is not the consequence of a fear of life or a sense of failure. Nārada was not an unaccomplished intellectual. His achievements were considerable and he had mastered nearly every discipline of his age. Maitreyī was not living in poverty. Yājñavalkya was leaving her with enough wealth to live a very comfortable life. Naciketas had the opportunity, with the blessings of Yama, to enjoy wealth, power, fame, pleasure, and long life. All three had reflected on the limits of their gains and accomplishments and yearned for something more enduring, meaningful, and satisfying. Arjuna's words in Bhagavadgītā (2:8) express well their predicament.

> Indeed, I do not see what should
> dispel
> This sorrow of mine which dries up
> the senses
> Though I should obtain on earth unrivalled and
> Prosperous royal power, or even the
> sovereignty of the gods.

This existential dissatisfaction, so common in the Hindu tradition, is a universal phenomenon. One of the best-known examples is the famous Russian author, Leo Tolstoy. At the pinnacle of his success, when he was wealthy, famous, and enjoyed the love of his family, Tolstoy was gripped by an unshakable sense of the meaninglessness of his life. All that he had formerly sought and found delight in seemed empty and insignificant. "All this," wrote Tolstoy, "took place at a time when so far as all my outward circumstances went, I ought to have been completely happy. I had a good wife who loved me and whom I loved; good children and a large property which was increasing with no pains taken on my part. I was more respected by my kinsfolk and acquaintance than I had ever been; I was loaded with praise by strangers; and without exaggeration I could believe my name already famous. . . . And yet, I could give no reasonable meaning to any actions of my life. . . . One can live only so long as one is intoxicated, drunk with life; but when one grows sober, one cannot fail to see that it is all a stupid cheat."[22]

What does the tradition advise for the person who experiences sorrow in the midst of pleasure, and want in the midst of plenty, and who struggles with an angst for meaning which cannot be assuaged by any worldly gain? The Muṇḍaka Upaniṣad (1.2.12) gives quite specific directions:

> A brahmin, after examining worldly gains achieved through action, understands that the uncreated cannot be created by finite action and becomes detached.
>
> To know that (the uncreated), he should go, with sacrifcial twigs in hand, to a teacher who knows the Vedas and who is established in *brahman.*[23]

This verse provides one of the clearest statements about the tradition's understanding of the fundamental human problem as well as the means for its resolution. A human being who engages in reflection on the nature of her actions and the outcomes produced, discovers that actions, which are by nature finite, are capable of producing only finite and hence limited results. One is still left, however grand one's attainments, in a state of want. The text also implies that at the heart of every human quest is a search for what it calls the uncreated (*akṛtah*). The uncreated is synonymous with the absolute or limitless, referred to, in the Upaniṣad, as *brahman.*[24] In other words, at the back of every finite search and action is a quest for the infinite and hence one of the reasons why the finite will always fail to satisfy. One comes to appreciate through the analysis of life experiences, with the help of the teacher, that one is aspiring for a reality that cannot be created through limited actions. This grasp of the limits of human action causes what the text refers to an attitude of detachment (*nirvedam*) from finite efforts and achievements. It is important to note here that the text does not completely negate the value and significance of human action in the world. Its aim is to comment on the limits of these in relation to the attainment of the limitless.

While such a discovery is likely to cause despair, its value from the Advaita viewpoint is unquestionable. As long as one does not appreciate the limits of the finite, one's expectations of its rewards will be unrealistic. One will seek from it more than it is capable of granting. Understanding its limits leads to an intellectual and emotional detachment that protects from despair. Dissatisfaction with the finite, in other words, is the beginning of the conscious journey to the infinite.

The Upaniṣad does not leave the seeker in despair. It affirms the possibility of gaining the limitless, the true object of human seeking, and, for this purpose, advises the student to approach a teacher (*guru*) who is learned in the scriptures (*śrotriyam*) and established in the limitless (*brahmaniṣṭham*). The student goes to the teacher "with twigs in hand." These twigs are meant for use in the teacher's ritual fire and indicate a humble readiness to serve the teacher during the learning process.

If we restated the human predicament in terms of traditional Hindu goals, we may say that the seeker has come to grasp the deficiencies of *artha* (wealth, power, and fame) and *kāma* (pleasure), and has awakened to the necessity of liberation (*mokṣa*) or an attainment that is free from the constraints of the finite. At this stage, one painfully knows the limits of finite gains and experiences, and has a yearning for something more enduring and fulfilling. A seeker, at this point in her quest, is traditionally referred to as a *jijñāsu* (one who desires knowledge) or a *mumukṣu* (one who desires liberation). "I have heard it said by your peers," Nārada told his teacher, Sanatkumāra, "that those who know the self pass across sorrow. Here I am, sir, a man full of sorrow. Please, sir, take me across to the other side of sorrow."[25] It is dissatisfaction with the finite and the desire to be free from sorrow that brings one to the door of a teacher.

CHAPTER TWO

The Requirements of Discipleship

THE NECESSITY OF VIRTUE

The Muṇḍaka Upaniṣad (1.2.13), which directs the student to seek out a teacher who is learned in the Vedas (*śrotriyaṁ*) and established in *brahman* (*brahmaniṣṭham*), also reminds the teacher, in the verse following immediately, of his obligations to the student.

> To that student who approaches in the proper manner, whose mind is calm and who is endowed with self-control, the wise teacher should fully impart the knowledge of *brahman*, through which one knows the true and imperishable Person.[1]

My purpose in citing the above verse is to draw attention to the emphasis, in the Upaniṣads, on the appropriate mental and emotional state, along with a corpus of values, that makes learning about the nature of *brahman* possible. The text mentions one with a calm mind (*praśāntacitta*) and self-control (*śamānvita*). The cultivation of basic moral values is an essential prerequisite for knowing *brahman* and this claim is reiterated throughout the Upaniṣads. The following are just a few of the direct statements in the Upaniṣads on the necessity for moral rectitude in the student:

> One who has not abstained from evil conduct, whose senses are not controlled and whose mind is not concentrated and calm cannot gain the Self through knowledge.[2]

> By truth this self can be grasped—
> by austerity, by right knowledge,
> and by a perpetually chaste life.
> It lies within the body, brilliant and full of light,
> which ascetics perceive,
> when their faults are wiped out.[3]

Moral rectitude is important for inquiry into the scripture, with the guidance of a qualified teacher, because of the uniqueness of the knowledge of *brahman.* The knowledge of *brahman,* referred to as *brahmajñāna,* shares a common feature with other kinds of knowledge. Like other knowledge, it takes place in the mind. Unlike other kinds of knowledge, however, *brahmajñāna* is concerned with the nature of the subject, the "I" who objectifies and knows everything. Where knowledge is concerned with realities other than the knower, it is not always necessary for the mind, the instrument of knowledge, to assume the nature of the object that it seeks to know. If a psychologist, for example, is studying the nature and causes of anger, she is not required to experience intense states of anger in her mind in order to understand the phenomena.[4] The object of inquiry is not the "I."

In the case of *brahman,* one is seeking to know a reality that is identical with one's self and whose nature is quite different from that which one customarily thinks of as one's self. *Brahman,* for example, is peace and stillness and cannot be known in a mind that does not enjoy these dispositions. A mind that is restless and in turmoil will not easily discern the still self. It is as difficult as trying to see the reflection of the moon that is present in a muddy and agitated container of water. *Brahman* exists equally and identically as the self of all, and such a truth can be grasped and celebrated only in a mind that is loving and compassionate. A hate-filled mind will not be interested or take delight in a teaching about the sameness of self.

In the matter of knowing *brahman,* knowledge is synonymous with being or becoming. "The knower of *brahman,*" as the Muṇḍaka Upaniṣad (3.2.9) states it, "becomes *brahman.*"[5] One is identical with that which one seeks to know or to be, and so the instrument of knowledge, the mind, must conform to the nature of the object of knowledge. A seeker after *brahman* must restrain the extrovert tendency of the mind and turn its attention inward. The qualifications required for inquiry in Advaita make such an inward turning possible. As Sara Grant rightly observes, "One cannot 'do' theology as one may 'do' mathematics or history or any other branch of academic study. Unless our life-style and value-systems are in harmony with the demands of the Truth we are pursuing, we cannot hope for real enlightenment."[6]

One who knows *brahman,* knows *brahman* to be the self of all. The consequence of such an understanding, as the Bhagavadgītā (6:29) puts it, is to see "the self present in all beings and all beings present in the self."[7] One grows to regard the sufferings and joys of others as one's own and becomes active in promoting and delighting in the well-being of others (*sarvabhūtahite ratāḥ*).[8] Since relationships of compassion and love are expressive of the knowledge of *brahman,* the one who aspires to such knowledge must also cultivate these virtues. A virtuous life, in other words, is both the means to as well as the expression of *brahmajñāna.* In his commentary on the Kena Upaniṣad, Śaṅkara observes "that the knowledge of *brahman* arises in a man who has attained the requisite holiness through purification of the heart." "For," continues Śaṅkara, "it is a matter of experience that, even though *brahman* is spoken of, there is either non-comprehension or mis-comprehension in the case of one who has not been purged of his sin. . . ."[9]

There is another reason for emphasizing the qualifications of the disciple. The knowledge of *brahman,* once gained, becomes meaningful only when retained in the mind. This is not true for other kinds of knowledge that do not concern the nature of one's self. To forget *brahman* is to forget the true nature of oneself. Such an unbroken recollection of the nature of oneself requires mindfulness and self-control. Whenever and for whatever reason the mind becomes forgetful of the self, it should be be gently led back to it. "By convincing oneself of the illusoriness of sense-objects through an investigation into their real nature," writes Śaṅkara, " and by cultivating indifference to worldly objects, the mind can be restrained from sense-objects and brought back to the Self wherein to abide firmly."[10]

The Advaita tradition has systematized and summarized the requirements of discipleship into four interrelated qualites or values. These are collectively referred to as the fourfold means (*sādhanacatuṣṭaya*) and include: *viveka, vairāgya, śamādiṣatkasampatti,* and *mumukṣutvam.* In his commentary on the *Brahmasūtra,* Śaṅkara refers to these requirements as, "discrimination between the eternal and the non-eternal; dispassion for the enjoyment of the fruits (of work) here and hereafter; a perfection of such practices as control of the mind, control of the sense organs, etc.; and a hankering for liberation."[11] We will consider each one in turn and comment on the interrelatedness of all four.[12]

VIVEKA

Viveka is the capacity to distinguish between the timeless (*nitya*) and the timebound (*anitya*). Advaita commentators generally elaborate by explaining that *viveka* is recognition that *brahman* alone is eternal and everything else is non-eternal. The problem here is that if a student, at the commencement of her study with a teacher, already understands and knows the eternal *brahman,* there is no need for further inquiry. *Viveka,* as the ability to distinguish the eternal from the non-eternal, is what one would expect from the student after the gain of knowledge.

At this initial stage, the student is endowed with *viveka* since she has assessed the various experiences of her life and has come to the conclusion that finite gains and accomplishments have an ultimately unsatisfactory character. She knows that lasting fulfillment cannot be found in the finite. In other words, while she may not yet know the eternal, she has reflected deeply on the non-eternal and its limits.

Viveka also suggests a capacity for rational inquiry and sustained reflection into the claims of the scriptures. The knowledge of *brahman* results from an inquiry (*jijñāsā*) into the nature of *brahman* as revealed in the scripture and interpreted by the teacher. Being a non-object, and being free from the characteristics that are normally used to define and describe entities in the world, both teacher and scripture use language in unusual ways to enable the student to grasp its reality. The Upaniṣads themselves speak of the necessity for a sharp and pointed mind.[13] An inquisitive, energetic, and alert mind is an asset to a student of *brahmajñāna.*

VAIRĀGYA

Vairāgya is freedom from longing for objects of enjoyment in this or other worlds. This outlook is a direct consequence of the conviction that non-eternal gains are ultimately unsatisfactory. *Vairāgya,* which is a healthy detachment from unrealistic expectations about finite gains and pleasures, arises from the exercise of *viveka. Vairāgya* is not a running away from the world because of fear or disgust. *Vairāgya* is a conviction born out of the understanding that while there are many legitimate worldly achievements and forms of enjoyment, there is a human need for meaning and fullness that these leave unsatisfied. A *virāgin* (one who possesses *vairāgya*) does not hate or condemn the world but enjoys life without greed and with detachment. T. M. P Mahadevan's characterization of *vairāgya* as " the disgust for seeing, hearing etc. of . . . non-eternal things," is a rather negative and antiworldly way of defining this value.[14]

Vairāgya is commonly associated with asceticism, mortification of the body, and the rejection of ordinary life in the world. Such practices and attitudes, however, often betray a lack of understanding about the fundamental human problem and its solution. A well-known portrait in the *Bhajagovindam* illustrates this misunderstanding.

> In front there is fire; at the back, there is the sun; in the night, (the ascetic sits) with the knees stuck to the chin; he receives alms in his palms, and lives under the trees; yet the bondage of desire does not leave him.[15]

The ascetic, described in this verse, warms himself with the heat of an inadequate fire at night and tries to stay comfortable by drawing his knees as close as possible to his chin. During the day, he relies on the heat of the sun. He owns no utensils for cooking or eating and is homeless. His renunciation, however, is merely outward, since his mind is still caught in the noose of greed (*tadpi na muñcatyāśāpāśaḥ*). Fleeing the objects of enjoyment, as the Bhagavadgītā reminds us, does not constitute *vairāgya,* since escapism does not liberate from greed.[16] Physical abstinence with mental indulgence and brooding is hypocritical:

> He who sits, restraining his power of
> Action,
> While in his mind brooding over
> The objects of the senses, with a
> deluded self,
> Is said to be a hypocrite.[17]

Preferable and superior to such self-deception is the freedom of a life in the world characterized by a detachment born of understanding.

Definitions of *vairāgya* also incorporate freedom from longing for objects of enjoyment in a heavenly world. The Advaita tradtition does not equate the attainment of heaven (*svarga*) with liberation (*mokṣa*). It accepts the possibility of the attainment of heavenly worlds after death as a consequence of the performance of meritorious actions, ethical and ritual. Arjuna, for example, in the Bhagavadgītā is promised the gain of heaven for his faithful performance of duty on the battlefield.[18] Since all actions are, by nature, finite, any gain produced as a consequence of such actions will also be finite. The heavenly worlds are no exception and one abides there for a limited time as determined by the nature of one's virtuous actions. When the good effects of these actions (*puṇya*) are exhausted through enjoyment, one returns to the world of mortality. "Having enjoyed," according to the Bhagavadgītā (9:21), "the vast world of heaven, they enter the world of mortals when their merit is exhausted."[19] The pleasures of heaven may vary in degree from those available here, but they are still finite and unsatisfactory. The fundamental human problem is not addressed by heavenly residence.

ŚAMĀDIṢATKASAMPATTI

The third requirement of discipleship is actually a group of six qualities referred to as the wealth of six disciplines (*śamādiṣatkasampatti*). These are *śama, dama, uparama, titikṣā, śraddhā,* and *samādhāna.*

Śama is the control or restraint of one's mind. A mind that has cultivated the qualities of *viveka* and *vairāgya* enjoys greater control. In the Bhagavadgītā 6:33–34, Arjuna raises, with his teacher, Kṛṣṇa, the problem of the mind's instability. He describes the mind as being turbulent, powerful, obstinate, and as difficult to restrain as the wind. While conceding that the mind is unsteady and difficult to restrain, Kṛṣṇa (6:35) recommends the regular practice of *vairāgya.* The restless character of the mind is, in part, a consequence of the human search for happiness. The mind moves from object to object, from gain to gain, in search of an elusive fulfillment. When one understands this predicament, one is in a better position achieve mastery over one's mind. The mind, as a result of established tendencies and habits, may be drawn to objects even when one has understood the temporal nature of these. A person who has cultivated the quality of *śama* is able to control the direction in which thought flows by the practice of reflecting on the limits of the finite. This technique is referred to as *pratipakṣa bhavana* or reflecting on the opposite. It is often necessary to repeat this until detachment toward the particular object is attained. The mental energies of a disciple lacking in *śama* are easily dissipated and she may find it very difficult to investigate the scriptures with the teacher, and to reason and reflect on their meaning.

Dama is the control of one's sense organs and organs of action and is an outcome of *śama.* The relationship between inward (*śama*) and outward control (*dama*) is beautifully considered in one of the famous analogies of the Kaṭha Upaniṣad (3:3–6). In this analogy, the body is likened to a chariot, reason to the charioteer, the mind to the reins, the senses to the horses, and the sense-objects to the roads. One who lacks understanding (*viveka*) and whose mind is consequently unrestrained loses control of his sense organs like the vicious horses of an unskillful charioteer. Where reason is enriched with wisdom, the mind is controlled and the senses are properly directed. One who achieves such control attains the goal of human existence (*mokṣa*). While *dama* should ideally follow from *śama,* there may be instances where one finds it difficult to check one's internal responses. *Dama,* however, ensures that these responses are kept at the mental level and do not find unpleasant and harmful expression in words and actions.

Uparama or *uparati* is the faithful observance of one's own duties.[20] In traditional Hindu society, one's duty (*dharma)* was defined primarily with reference to one's stage (*āśrama*) of life and one's place in the caste (*varṇa*) system. The social system resulting from the integration of these two orders is known as *varṇāśramadharma.* The four stages are those of the student (*brahmacarya*), householder (*gṛhastya*), forest-dweller (*vānaprasthya*), and renunciation (*sannyāsa*). The four *varṇas* consist of priests and teachers (*brahmins*), rulers and warriors (*kṣatriyas*), merchants and farmers (*vaiśyas*), and laborers and servants *(śūdras*). Each stage and caste had its defined duties.[21] The social order was essentially conservative in character since membership in a *varṇa* was usually determined by birth and faithful adherence to duty emphasized as a requirement of religious growth. The system also led to the creation of a large group of outcastes who were considered ritually impure and denied the opportunities and privileges enjoyed by members of the four *varṇas.*

In contemporary Hindu society, however, the social order is in transition and duty is not always defined with reference to stage in life and caste. Occupational choices are less limited by birth. The rich concept of duty, however, which incorporates dedicated performance of one's work and the notion of work as obligatory offering, is not inextricably bound to the system of *varṇāśramadharma.* It can enrich and enhance the meaning of work that is freely chosen. The significance of *uparama* as a requirement of discipleship is that work in the world is not necessarily incompatible with the quest for liberation, and must be carried out with a sense of sanctity and obligation.[22]

Titikṣā is defined as the ability to endure life's opposites. It is an acknowledgment of the shifting dualistic nature of reality. Experiences of pain and pleasure, gain and loss, comfort and discomfort are a part of the fabric of life and one has to discover the ability to maintain an equilibrium in the midst of them all. *Titikṣā* is not an unemotional inability to discern the difference between a pleasant outcome or experience and an unpleasant one. One should be able to delight in a desired outcome with a poise and wisdom that an undesirable outcome does not shatter. One knows the limits of all finite experiences, pleasant and unpleasant, and refuses to be distracted by any one of them in the quest for *brahman.* "Physical sensations," says Kṛṣṇa in Bhagavadgītā (2:14), "causing cold, heat, pleasure or pain, come and go and are impermanent. . . . Endure (*titikṣasva*) them."[23]

Śraddhā is faith in meaning of the scripture as taught by the teacher.[24] A student goes to a teacher after scrutinizing the finite gains that are possible through human action and with a conviction about the inability of any of these to satisfy the deepest human wants and longings. She approaches the teacher after hearing that there is a wisdom that resolves the fundamental human problem. *Śraddhā* is freedom from cynicism about life and is a commitment to inquiry with the teacher's guidance. A deep-rooted skepticism about the teacher or the scripture makes it impossible to patiently undertake any inquiry. *Śraddhā,* however, should not be construed as implying an unthinking obedience and acceptance of everything required and taught by one's teacher.[25] While truth about the ultimate may not be entirely accessible through the independent operations of human reason, the search for it does not require the suspension or abandonment of human rationality. The Upaniṣads commend the role of the human intellect in the process of inquiring into *brahman.*[26]

Samādhāna is the ability to focus the mind on a particular enterprise or field of activity without being easily distracted. For the Advaita student, this means dedication to the task of listening, reasoning, and contemplating on the meaning of the scripture. Distractions ought to be minimal for someone who is endowed with *viveka* and *vairāgya* and who has developed self-control. Since the world of finitude does not offer the fullness that she seeks, she is ready to consider and energetically pursue the Vedantic alternative. *Samādhāna* is generally equated with *citta ekāgratā* or single-pointedness of mind.

MUMUKṢUTVA

The fourth and final qualification for discipleship is *mumukṣutva.* This is an intense desire for liberation *(mokṣa*), arising, as we have seen, from a personal discovery of the fact that the fulfillment of desires for the finite does not resolve one's experience of want and dissatisfaction. One who is motivated by a desire for liberation is called a *mumukṣu.* The student, like Nārada, experiences the reality of sorrow and yearns for a way of overcoming it. Her interest in the scripture and teacher is not the expression of a detached curiosity. She goes to the teacher with an ardent hope that he teaches a wisdom and way across suffering. Sadānanda describes the student as approaching the teacher in the same manner that one whose head is on fire rushes to a lake.[27] In the absence of *mumukṣutva,* exposure to the scripture and teacher will have minimal personal significance. The wisdom of the scriptures comes with the impact and revelation of a solution only when the predicament of a life is brought before it with faith.

One who exemplifies the above fourfold means is eligible for inquiry into the Vedānta. She becomes an *adhikārin,* that is, a qualified student for the knowledge of *brahman.* It should be emphasized here that Advaita does not require the perfection of the fourfold means as a precondition for inquiry into *brahman.* As one understands and becomes centered in *brahman,* one's understanding of these values and their expression in one's life also grow and deepen. They manifest in one's thinking and behavior in a more spontaneous manner. A seeker must be aware of these values and their importance and strive diligently to express them in her thinking and conduct.

SĀDHANA CATUṢṬAYA AND THE IMMEDIACY OF KNOWLEDGE

The knowledge of *brahman,* in the Advaita tradition, is not objective information about *brahman.* It is knowledge about the fundamental nature of the seeker. The fruit of knowledge is discovering one's identity with *brahman,* overcoming sorrow and attaining immortality. Muṇḍaka Upaniṣad (3.2.9), as it concludes, summarizes the consequences of *brahmajñāna.*

> When a man comes to know that highest *brahman,* he himself becomes that very *brahman.* A man without the knowledge of *brahman* will not be born in his family. He passes beyond sorrow, he passes beyond evil. Freed from the knots of the heart, he will become immortal.[28]

The Kaṭha Upaniṣad (6:18) also concludes with a praise and summary of the results of *brahmajñāna.*

> Then after Naciketas received this body of knowledge,
> and the entire set of yogic rules taught by Death,
> He attained *brahman;* he became free from aging and death;
> so will others who know this teaching about the self.[29]

The emphasis in the Upaniṣads is on the immediate attainment of *brahman,* immortality, and freedom from sorrow as a consequence of knowledge. These immediate results are possible for the disciple, such as Naciketas, who comes to the teacher and scripture endowed with the fourfold qualifications. Such a disciple can proclaim with delight, like the students at the end of the Praśna Upaniṣad (6.8) to their teacher, Pippalāda, "You are, indeed, our father, for you have taken us to the farthest shore beyond ignorance." For a disciple with the fourfold qualifications, and particularly with faith (*śraddhā*), the scripture functions, as it is meant to do in the Advaita understanding, as an immediate and valid source of knowledge about *brahman.* A contemporary Advaita Vedānta teacher compares scripture to the eyes and emphasizes that even "as eyes are not an aid to seeing but are the means by which one sees, so, too the words of the Vedānta are not an aid to knowing oneself but are the very means by which one knows oneself. Vedānta is not an aid which makes it *easier* to understand the nature of oneself thorough some other means. Vedānta *is* the means. The words of the Vedānta *are* the instrument for knowing oneself just as the eye is the instrument for seeing."[30]

The traditional emphasis on the requirements of discipleship is explicable in a context where the human problem was recognized and treated seriously as an existential problem and where the scripture enjoyed the status of a valid means of knowledge capable, in the hands of a learned and liberated teacher, of freeing from sorrow. It is common, therefore, for the Upaniṣads to conclude by identifying the eligible disciple. The Śvetāśvatara Upaniṣad (6:22–23), for example, concludes with the following verses:

> This highest Vedānta secret, expounded in a former age, should not be given to one who is not tranquil, or to an unworthy son or an unworthy disciple.
>
> These truths shine only when expounded to the great soul who has supreme devotion to God and for the teacher.[31]

Muṇḍaka Upaniṣad (3.2.10) concludes with the following instructions about teaching:

> Who are versed in the Vedas and perform rites,
> Who are grounded in *brahman,*
> Who offer for themselves, with faith in the lone seer,
> to these alone let a man teach
> this knowledge of *brahman*
> So long as they have duly performed the head-vow.[32]

ELIGIBILITY FOR DISCIPLESHIP AND THE CASTE SYSTEM

A major problem, however, with the orthodox understanding of eligibility or competence (*adhikāra*) to inquire into the Upaniṣads is that it has been interpreted with reference to *varṇāśramadharma.* Within the confines of this worldview, eligibility for Vedic study was limited to male members of the first three castes. Women and *śudras* were excluded, as well as the untouchables who were without caste. The fourfold qualifications, in other words, were not overlooked, but interpreted within the hierarchy and privileges of the caste system. Excluding large groups on the basis of birth criterion and not strictly on the basis of the fourfold requirement thus circumscribed the universality of the latter. In the *Upadeśasāhasrī* (II.I.1), for instance, Śaṅkara, emphasizes the fourfold requirements along with the stipulation that the student must be of the *brahmin* caste.

> The means to final release is knowledge [of *Brahman*]. It should be repeatedly related to the pupil until it is firmly grasped, if he is dispassionate toward all things non-eternal which are attained by means [other than knowledge]; if he has abandoned the desire for sons, wealth, and the worlds and reached the state of a *paramahaṁsa,* wandering ascetic.; if he is endowed with tranquility, self-control, compassion, and so forth; if he is possessed of the qualities of a pupil which are well known from the scriptures; if he is a Brahmin who is

> [internally and externally] pure; if he approaches his teacher in the prescribed manner; if his caste, profession, behavior, knowledge [of the *Veda*], and family have been examined.

Śaṅkara clearly upholds the traditional social order of *varṇāśramavyavasthā* and rejects the rights of *śūdras* to study the Vedas. "The *śūdra,*" according to Śaṅkara, "has no competence, since he cannot study the Vedas; for one becomes competent for things spoken of in the Vedas, after one has studied the Vedas and known these things from them. But there can be no reading of the Vedas by a *śūdra,* for Vedic study presupposes the investiture with the sacred thread, which ceremony is confined to the three castes."[33] Śaṅkara quotes, with approval, passages from a variety of Hindu authoritative writings supporting the exclusion of the *śūdras* from hearing, study, and knowing the meaning of the Vedas.

> As for prohibition of hearing, we have the text, "Then should he happen to hear the Vedas, the expiation consists in his ears being filled with lead and lac," and "He who is a *śūdra* is a walking crematorium. Hence one should not read in the neighbourhood of a *śūdra.* From this follows the prohibition about study. How can one study the Vedas when they are not to be recited within his hearing? Then there is the chopping off of his tongue if he should utter the Vedas and the cutting of the body to pieces if he should commit it to memory.[34]

Śaṅkara does allow *śūdras* the opportunity for liberating knowledge but this may be acquired indirectly by hearing through texts that are secondary in authority and status to the Vedas, such as the *Ītihāsa* and *Purāṇa.* While such a concession may be commendable, one must still wonder about the reality of *śūdras* having access to liberating knowledge through secondary texts. Do we have any examples? Control of these texts would still remain in the hands of *brahmins*, and *śūdras* would continue to be subservient and dependent. While it is true, as Michael Comans argues, that Śaṅkara's position reflects the conditions of his time, criticism of inequality does not only reflect "the vantage point of our times when the principle of political equality, stemming from the European Enlightenment, is now widely accepted as a moral right."[35] Criticism of caste inequality, as far as the knowledge of *brahman* is concerned, can also find justification in the Advaita teaching about the identity and sameness of self in all beings. It remains a matter of concern that the greatest historical exponent of this teaching remained untroubled by social inequality, a contradiction that is still not uncommon. There is still a tendency to offer mild explanations for Śaṅkara's attitude.[36]

In the light of the universality of the human problem which Advaita addresses and in view of its claim that the Upaniṣads are a valid source of knowledge for addressing and resolving this problem, it is necessary for the tradition to emphasize an eligibility that is centered on the fourfold requirements and to sever the connection between these requirements and the traditional caste system. It is helpful to note the fact that the fourfold means do not contain any stipulations about caste and that Śaṅkara does not deny the ability of members of the so-called lower castes to gain liberating knowledge. He denies them the right to Vedic study but not to *brahmajñāna.*

The fourfold requirement must also be liberated from the prejudices and power hierarchies of patriarchy. These requirements share a great deal with the demands of the religious path in many traditions and their disconnection from the caste order and patriarchy would enhance the rationality and human claims of the Vedānta. Human beings everywhere experience the existential meaninglessness of a Nārada or the discontent with wealth of a Maitreyī and this, more than anything else, entitles them to the opportunity for Advaita inquiry. The liberation of Advaita from the constraints of a conservative social and ritual order will not only enhance its universality, but will also unleash its potential to challenge the social and religious inequities of caste and gender. There is a need, today, for the monastic orders and institutions associated with the tradition of Advaita to explicitly and formally renounce eligibility that is based on caste and gender and articulate an interpretation of Vedantic eligibility that is centered solely on the fourfold means discussed above. There are rich resources within the tradition for doing so, but it requires also a willingness to self-critically admit historical and contemporary injustices of caste and gender and to subject Śaṅkara's endorsement to rigorous historical criticism.

CHAPTER THREE

The Nature of the *Ātman*

The basic problem of human beings, according to the Advaita Vedānta tradition, is that the experience of the finite and the satisfaction of desires for wealth and pleasure leave us wanting. Secular knowledge, as Nārada discovered, also culminates in the discontent of sorrow. Even the more intangible gains such as fame, power, and social prestige leave us with a sense of incompleteness. The multiplication of desires does not liberate us from want. Satisfactions are ephemeral and behind everything "is the great spectre of death, the all encompassing blackness."[1]

The desire for a wisdom that satisfies the human longing for meaning and fullness underlies the question of Śaunaka to his teacher, Aṅgiras, at the beginning of the Muṇḍaka Upaniṣad (1.3). "What is it, my lord, by knowing which one comes to understand everything?"[2] Śaunaka's question is not a request for empirical information about the world. It is a desire for meaning in existence, a solution to the despair of his own life. The students at the beginning of the Śvetāśvatara Upaniṣad (1.1) ask a series of questions centered on the meaning of their lives. Why were we born? By what do we live? On what are we established? These are universal human questions concerning the origin, purpose, and goal of human existence.[3] In Maitreyī's question to her husband, Yājñavalkya, "If I were to possess the entire world filled with wealth, would it make me immortal?" we find expression of the human anxiety about mortality and a longing for the transcendence of death. In the case of Nārada, his vast learning and attainments did not bring him lasting happiness. He spoke of the human predicament by confessing to his teacher that he is a "man full of sorrow," and requests to be liberated from his suffering. His sorrow is born of a persistent experience of incompleteness.

OVERCOMING THE HUMAN PROBLEM

The human problem expresses itself in a variety of modes: as a longing for meaning, the fear of death, or the sorrow of an unfulfilled life. At the back of it, according to the Upaniṣads, is the desire for the infinite. In the view of the Upaniṣads, it is the attainment or gain of the infinite that truly resolves the human problem. "Only when people," says the teacher in the Śvetāśvatara Upaniṣad (6:23), "will be able to roll up the sky like a piece of leather will suffering come to end, without first knowing God." "It is the infinite," says Sanatkumāra to Nārada in the Chāndogya Upaniṣad (7.23.1), " that is bliss. There is no bliss in the finite. Only the infinite is bliss. One must desire to know the infinite." The infinite is immortal whereas the finite is mortal.[4]

The infinite is referred to in the Upaniṣads as *brahman* and the knowledge of *brahman* (*brahmavidyā* or *brahmajñāna*) liberates the seeker from the human predicament of meaninglessness, sorrow, and fear of mortality. "I know," says the teacher in the Śvetāśvatara Upaniṣad (3:8), "that Infinite Being, shining like the sun and beyond all darkness. Only by knowing him does one pass beyond death; there is no other path."[5]

How does the teacher in the Upaniṣads instruct the student about the nature of *brahman*? The gist of the Upaniṣadic solution to the human problem is to point out that the seeker is the sought. In other words, one is already the immortal and full being that one desires to become. The self (I) (*ātman*) is the infinite (*brahman*). This truth is summarized in what the Advaita tradition regards as the four great Upaniṣadic sentences (*mahāvākyas*). These are as follows: "That Thou Art (*tat tvam asi*)" is taken from the Chāndogya Upaniṣad (6.8.7) of the Sāma Veda; "This *ātman* is *brahman* (*ayam ātma brahma*)" is taken from the Māṅḍukya Upaniṣad (2) of the Atharva Veda; "Consciousness is *brahman* (*prajñānaṁ brahma*)" is taken from Aitareya Upaniṣad (5.3) of the Ṛg Veda; and "I am *brahman* (*ahaṁ brahmāsmi*)" is taken from Bṛhadāraṇyaka Upaniṣad (1.4.10) of the Yajur Veda.

If one is not different from the limitless, and if one still seeks the limitless, then the problem may be understood as one of self-ignorance (*avidyā*) and the tradition is replete with numerous parables illustrating this predicament. A famous one, used by Śaṅkara himself, is the story of the tenth person.[6] Ten disciples were on their way to a sacred site when they encountered a river in flood. Not finding a boatman, they decided to swim across the rapid waters. After reaching the opposite shore, the leader took a count to ascertain whether everyone was safe. To his dismay, one appeared to be missing. Each disciple repeated the count and came up with the same result—the tenth person was lost. This loss caused sadness and a feeling of helplessness. A woodcutter, attracted by their wailing, became curious and inquired about their predicament. After patiently listening, he requested the leader to repeat his count. When he stopped at nine, the stranger asked why he had not included himself in the count. "You are the tenth person!" exclaimed the woodcutter, bursting into laughter. The students immediately understood the problem and their grief vanished. The tenth person, lost in ignorance, was discovered to be always there.

The sense of separation from *brahman* is described as a problem of ignorance about one's true nature and this results in the assumption of a false identity. Śaṅkara recounts the story of a prince who was abandoned by his parents at birth and raised in a fowler's home. Ignorant of his identity as a prince and heir to his father's throne, he thought of himself as a fowler's son and learned to trap birds. A compassionate person (viz., the *guru*), who knew of the boy's royal identity, explained to him that he was not a fowler, but the son of a king and that his current identity was not his true one. The boy gave up the notion of being a fowler and the duties associated with that identity and assumed his princely identity and activities.[7] In another well-known illustration from the Chāndogya Upaniṣad (6.14.1), the person under the condition of ignorance is likened to someone forcefully taken from his beloved home, blindfolded, and left in a place of desolation. A kind person answers his cries for help, removes his blindfold, and shows him the way to his home. In a similar manner, says Śaṅkara, a merciful teacher liberates the *avidyā*-bound individual by pointing out his identity with the limitless *brahman*.[8]

WHO AM I?

If one's identity, as in the above parables, is different from what one assumes it to be, the question, "Who am I?" becomes central to the Advaita inquiry and teachers make it the focus of their pedagogy. One of the most skilful in the use of this technique was the South Indian teacher Ramana Maharshi (1879–1950), who always brought inquirers back to this fundamental issue. Questioned about life after death, for example, Ramana might reply, "Why do you want to know what you will be when you die before you know what you are now? First find out what you are now." Questions about God were similarly treated. "Why do you want to know about God before you know about yourself?"[9]

The common method used by teachers of Advaita to help students appreciate the nature of the "I" (*ātman*) is the introspective technique of distinguishing between the "knower" and the "known" or the "subject" and "object." This is popularly referred to as *dṛg-dṛśya viveka*, or inquiry into the nature of the "seer" and "seen." The various answers that one may give to the question "Who are you?" are regarded by Advaita as relative and practically useful, but not definitive of the nature of the self. A name, for example, is a necessary label that identifies a person in community of similar beings. It does not, however, define a person's fundamental nature since one may change one's name and yet be essentially the same person. One exists, even without a name. Similarly, while work is an important dimension of the meaning of our lives, defining the self through one's work is relative in nature. It tells what one does, but not what one is. It describes the nature of the work, but not the nature of the one who works. If one changes one's profession, retires, or becomes unemployed, the self still is. The importance of this method of distinguishing the subject from the object is underlined by Śaṅkara's use of it to begin his commentary on the *Brahmasūtra*.

> It being an established fact that the object and the subject, that are fit to be the contents of the concepts "you" and "we" (respectively), and are by nature as contradictory as light and darkness, cannot logically have any identity, it follows that their attributes can have it still less. Accordingly, the superimposition of the object, referable through the concept of "you," and its attributes on the subject that is conscious by nature and is referable through the concept "we" and contrariwise the superimposition of the subject and its attributes on the object should be impossible. Nevertheless, owing to an absence of discrimination between the attributes, as also between substances, which are absolutely disparate, there continues a natural human behaviour based on self-identification in the form of "I am this" or "This is mine."[10]

The importance of human relationships is reflected in the ways in which these inform our self-definitions. I may describe myself as a husband, son, brother, uncle, nephew, disciple, or friend depending on the particular context. All of these tell about me in relation to someone else and explain the intricate web of relations in which I am involved and the many human roles that I play. If the self is absolutely any one of these, claims Advaita, it cannot be anyone or anything else. In order to assume all of these roles, the self has to be, in some sense, different from any particular one. Like an actor on stage, its ability to assume different roles depends on it not being absolutely identified with any particular one. What is the nature of the "I" independent of name, profession, and relationships? Here is where the method of distinguishing between the "knower" and "known" becomes helpful.

With reference to things in the world, it is not difficult to appreciate that the *ātman* is different from any one of these since they are objectified through the senses and the mind. The nature of the self as a knower in relation to the tree outside one's window is obvious. One does not normally identify oneself with the tree. Even when one identifies oneself with an external object, one is aware of using a figurative mode of speech. A driver, for example, may boast to her friends, "I did a hundred miles per hour on the highway," but does not seriously think of herself as identical with her car. In terms of "knower" and "known," the self is the "knower" and the car is "known." The self is the subject and things in the world fall into the category of objects.

THE *ĀTMAN* AND THE BODY

Advaita takes this mode of inquiry another step farther and asks us to consider the relationship between the self and the physical body. It is apparent that while a person may not literally identify herself with an external object, she does have a deeply rooted I-sense in the body.[11] It is quite normal to identify oneself with all the attributes of one's physical body, such as height, color, and weight. On the basis of identity between the self and the body, one thinks of oneself as a mortal being subject to birth, growth, change, and eventual death. But, the Advaita teacher asks, "Is this physical body known or not?"[12] When one speaks of oneself as being tall or white, the body is perceived and objectified. Like other objects in the world, the body is seen and felt and its attributes known. By the fact that one is aware of one's body, and that it belongs to the category of the "known," the body is not regarded to be the same as the "I." The technical expression used in Advaita for the identification of the self with the body is *dehātmabuddhi*. This is the false conclusion that the self (*ātma*) is the body (*deha*).[13]

If the self is not identical with the physical body, is it the same as the sense organs through which one sees, hears, touches, tastes, and smells? A person may regard the self as being blind when her eyes are nonfunctional. The identification between the self and the senses is articulated in statements such as, " I am blind," or "I am deaf." In these cases, a defect of the sense organ is superimposed on the self.[14] The Advaita teacher asks the same question about the sense organs and the body. "Are the senses known or not?" The senses and their respective conditions are obviously known. If one's eyes are blind or defective in any manner, this condition is known. One is aware of the senses, just as one is aware of one's body, and these are not to be identified with the *ātman*.

Advaita does not regard the five senses as independent centers of awareness or experience. In other words, it is not accurate to think that the eyes see, the ears hear, the tongue tastes, the skin feels, and the nose smells. The senses are considered to be the instruments through which the one conscious self sees, hears, smells, etc. It is the distinctness of the self from any particular sense organ that enables the same experiencer to have multiple sense experiences of one object. One can see, smell, taste, and touch the same apple. It is to convey the idea that the senses are not separate centers of experience that the Kena Upaniṣad (1.1) describes the self as "eye of the eye" and the "ear of the ear." In his commentary on the Bṛhadāraṇyaka Upaniṣad (4.4.18) Śaṅkara notes that the "eye and other organs receive their powers of vision and so forth only by being inspired by the energy of *brahman;* by themselves, divested of the light of the *ātman* that is Pure Intelligence, they are like wood or clods of earth."

THE *ĀTMAN* AND THE MIND

If the "I" is not identical with the body or the senses, is it identical with the mind? It is obvious that the presence of the mind is necessary for the proper operation of the senses. A healthy ear fails to apprehend sounds within its range unless it is conjoined with an attentive mind. The same is true for the other senses. The identification of the self and the mind is expressed in statements such as, "I am angry," "I am restless," or "I am satisfied." Mental states, however, are all known and are objects of one's awareness. The self knows them as they arise through a process of internal cognition, which does not require the senses to function as intermediaries. In addition, mental states generally have a transient character about them. Each state occupies the mind for a limited time before giving way to other states. If the self is identical with any particular mental state such as fear, hate, doubt, delight, or mistrust, it would come into being only when the particular emotion was aroused and would cease to be with its passing. The Kena Upaniṣad (1.5) points to the nature of the mind as an object of the self when it describes the self as that "which one cannot grasp with one's mind, by which they say the mind itself is grasped."[15]

It is important to note here that while the Sanskrit term *manas* is commonly translated as mind, technically speaking *manas* is one mode of a more comprehensive internal organ referred to as the *antaḥkaraṇa* and which has four functions (*vṛtti*). *Manas* is the function of deliberation or the weighing of pros and cons, *buddhi* is the function of determination and decision making, *citta* is the function of memory or recollection, and *ahaṁkāra* is the ego or "I" thought. It is not uncommon for the terms *manas, buddhi,* or *citta* to be used for the entire internal organ. All four modes of the mind are known. One is aware of deliberation, decision, memories, and the I-notion and all four are regarded as different from the self.

THE *ĀTMAN* AS AWARENESS

In relation to the body, sense organs, mind (*manas*), intellect (*buddhi*), memory (*citta*), and ego (*ahaṁkāra*), the "I" is the knower or the subject. All of these are in constant change and are objects of knowledge. What then is the nature of the *ātman*?

I am *aware* / of my body.
I am *aware* / of my senses.
I am *aware* / of my mind.
I am *aware* / of my memories.
I am *aware* / of my ego.

With reference to the various objects of knowledge, the appropriate way of describing the *ātman* is as an awarer. This term, however, implies the objects of which the self is aware. How may we describe the self without reference to any objects of knowledge? From this standpoint, it may be appropriate to describe the self as awareness.

Swami Dayananda Sarsawati justifies the description of the self as awareness, and not as awarer, through the following argument:

> Are you the awarer always, or are you the awarer only with reference to the things of which you are aware? Just as you are a seer with reference to objects seen, a hearer with reference to sounds heard, a taster with reference to tastes, you are an awarer only with reference to the objects of which you are aware. Without reference to objects, with reference only to yourself, you are the content of the awarer. That essence can only be Awareness.[16]

As awareness, the self illumines and objectifies the body, mind, and all things that are known. In itself, however, it cannot be objectified. To objectify the self, another self would be necessary. A second self does not exist, and the self cannot be both subject and object. "As fire does not burn itself," writes Śaṅkara in his commentary on the *Bṛhadāraṅyaka Upaniṣad* 2.4.14, "the self does not know itself, and the knower can have no knowledge of a thing that is not its object. Therefore, through what instrument should one know the knower owing to which this universe is known and who else should know it?" In a well-known Advaita text, *Dṛg Dṛśya Viveka,* the author opens with a verse indicating the nature of the *ātman* as illumining awareness and as not available for objectification.[17] The verse is also expounding a traditional method of instruction for teaching that the self is nonobjectifiable awareness.

> The form is perceived and the eye is the perceiver. It (eye) is perceived and the mind is the perceiver. The mind with its modifications is perceived and the Witness (the self) is the perceiver. But It (the Witness) is not perceived (by any other).

In this verse, forms represent all sense objects and the eye includes all sense organs. Sense objects are objectified by the senses, the senses are objectified by the mind and the self objectifies the various states of the mind. The self is always the knower and never an object of knowledge (*dṛgeva na tu dṛśyate*). It is extremely important to distinguish the self from the agent of knowing or the ego. Śaṅkara emphasizes this in his commentary on *Taittirīya Upaniṣad* (2.1), *satyaṁ jñānam anantam brahma* (*brahman is Being, Awareness, Limitless*). The juxtaposition of the words *satya* (Being) and *ananta* (Limitless) with *jñāna* (Awareness) removes the finitude of the ego that is subject to change and points to the underlying self as unlimited awareness.

> The word *jñāna* conveys the abstract notion of the verb, *jña,* to know; and being an attribute of *brahman* along with truth and infinitude, it does not indicate the agent of knowing. If *brahman* be the agent of knowing, truth and infinitude cannot justly be attributed to It. For as the agent of knowing, It becomes changeful; and, as such, how can It be true and infinite?

An often-cited sequence of verses in the first chapter of the *Kena Upaniṣad* also treats the nature of the self as ultimate subject in relation to the mind and senses.

> Which one cannot grasp with one's mind,
> by which, they say, the mind itself is grasped—
> Know that that alone is *brahman,*
> and not what they here meditate.
>
> Which one cannot see with one's sight,
> by which one sees the sight itself—

Know that that alone is *brahman*,
and not what they here meditate.

Which one cannot hear with one's hearing,
by which hearing itself is heard—
Know that that alone is *brahman*,
and not what they here meditate.[18]

Following on the discussion in second chapter of the Taittirīya Upaniṣad, Advaita distinguishes the self from what is referred to as the five-sheaths (*pañca kośa*), and the physical, subtle, and causal bodies.[19] These are a more detailed subdivision of the body, mind, and senses. They are called sheaths, since they envelop the self in the same manner that its sheath may enclose a sword. The sheaths are successively subtler in character and are arranged one within the other in a telescopic manner.

The outermost is the *annamaya kośa,* or food sheath. It is called the food sheath because the body is composed of, sustained by, and perishes without food. The *annamaya kośa* corresponds to the physical body, or *sthūla śarīra*, that is understood to be composed of five elements, space, air, heat, water, and minerals, in their tangible or manifest forms, which are available for perception and experience through the sense organs. The next three sheaths, the vitality sheath (*prāṇamaya kośa*), the mind sheath (*manomaya kośa*), and the intellect sheath (*vijñānamaya kośa*), comprise the subtle body, or *sūkṣma śarīra.* The subtle body is constituted of the same five elements as the physical body, but in their uncompounded or subtle forms.[20] Because of its fine or subtle character, it is not destroyed with the death of the physical body.

The vitality sheath animates the physical body and expresses itself functionally in five ways. These are in respiration (*prāṇa*), excretion (*apāna*), circulation (*vyāna*), ejection (*udāna*), especially in bringing about the separation of the physical and subtle bodies at the time of death, and digestion (*samāna*). The mind sheath (*manomaya kośa*) and the intellect sheath (*vijñāmaya kośa*) refer, as earlier indicated, to the deliberative and determinative functions of the internal organ (*antaḥkaraṇa*).

The fifth sheath, the bliss sheath (*ānandamaya kośa*) corresponds to the causal body, or *kāraṇa śarīra.* It manifests itself particularly in the deep sleep state when all mental and emotional phenomena enter into a seed-like or dormant state. From this causal condition, they emerge and become active in the waking and dream states. The bliss sheath is so called because deep sleep is characterized by an experience of happiness or nonawareness of limitation. The *ātman* is distinct from the five sheaths and the three bodies, which are all objects of awareness.

THE *ĀTMAN* AS TIMELESS

The self that is thus understood in Advaita to be nonobjectifiable awareness, is also regarded as free from the limits of time. It exists in all three periods of time, past, present, and future. Objects that are limited by time are subject to modifications of six kinds: birth, existence (after birth), growth, transformation, decline, and death. Advaita denies all these with reference to the self.[21] Bhagavadgītā (2:12–25) offers a lengthy discussion on the theme of the immortality and indestructibility of the self. "Truly," Kṛṣṇa (2:12) assures Arjuna, "there was never a time when I was not, nor you, nor these lords of men; and neither will there be a time when we shall cease to be. All of us transcend this time."[22] All possible forms of destruction are ruled out for the self. It is not dismembered by weapons, burnt by fire, drowned in water, or dried up by the winds.[23]

In order to help his student, Arjuna, understand the continuity of the self in time, Kṛṣṇa (2:13) challenges him to reflect on the common human experience of growth.

> Just as in the body childhood, adulthood, and senescence happen to the embodied one, so also it (the embodied being) acquires another body. The wise one, in this, is not deluded.

In the movement from childhood, adulthood, and old age, our physical bodies undergo significant changes. Our experiences in these stages also differ and our memories are consequently varied. Is there anything constant in these stages of growth? The constant factor, suggests Kṛṣṇa, is the self as awareness. In childhood, one is aware of one's childhood body. This body "dies," in a manner of speaking, and makes way for an adult body. One is now aware of one's adult body and of having lived in a child's body. When the adult body gives way to an old body, one will be aware of one's aged body and of having lived in a child's body and an adult's body. Bodies and the experiences associated with these vary, but in each one the self as awareness exists. It does not cease to be when the body changes. The recollection, in old age, of the childhood and adult bodies indicates that the one dwelling in the old body is the same one who lived in the child and adult bodies. Bodies, at various stages, may be thought of as different suits of clothing that the same wearer uses and changes.[24] As awareness, the *ātman* makes known and illumines all changes in the body and mind. It is that because of which time itself is known and is thus not regarded as subject to time and change.

Advaita also finds support for its understanding of the self as constant and timeless awareness through the analysis of the three states of experience, waking, dreaming, and sleeping (*avasthātraya*). This analysis is traditionally referred to as *avasthātraya vicara* and is based, in particular, on the Māṇḍūkya Upaniṣad. In the waking state (*jāgradavasthā*), one is conscious of the physical world through the mind, senses, and the body. Awarenesss is externally oriented (*bahiṣprajña*). We must recollect here that the body, senses, and mind are instruments for the self. There can be no physical or sense experiences and no thinking process without awareness. To read the words on the pages of this book, for example, the eyes function as the instrument of seeing, but the seer is the self.

In the dream state (*svapnāvasthā*), awareness is internally oriented (*antaḥ prajña).* In contrast to the waking state where the self, through the mind and body, experiences the physical world, the dream experience is one of subtle or mind-created objects. It is in the light of awareness, however, that the entire dream experience occurs and is experienced. It is the same awareness because of which the waking world is experienced.

The third state is that of dreamless sleep (*suṣuptyavasthā*). Here, one is not aware of the physical world of the waking state or the subtle world of the dream state. The sleeper is free from desires for enjoyment and has no experience of physical or mental pleasure and pain born out of contact from an object. Advaita, however, contends that the self as awareness is present also in the deep sleep state. The state is not regarded as one of unawareness or unconsciousness. The testimony, on awakening from dreamless sleep that, "I slept very well, I did not know anything," is regarded by Advaita as a matter of direct experience in the state of sleep. Awareness, in other words, is present in deep sleep, but it is an awareness of the absence of physical and mental phenomena.

The objects of the waking world give way to the subtle objects of the dream world and both give way to the experience of noncognition in sleep. In all three states, Advaita contends, *ātman* (I) as awareness is common and constant. The self in the waking state is the same in the dream and deep sleep states as evidenced by the continuity of memory. At this moment, you are reading these words in the waking state. Tonight you may have the experiences of dream and dreamless sleep. Tomorrow morning, you may recollect the experiences of all three states. The contents of the three states are subject to change, "But underlying them and persisting throughout is the Self. The 'I' that was there in the waking state, was also there in the dream and deep-sleep states. The states pass and vary, but the underlying consciousness remains the same."[25]

THE *ĀTMAN* AS *ĀNANDA*

The Upaniṣads use the term *ānanda* to describe *brahman.* The English term most widely used for translating *ānanda* is "bliss." In the Bṛhadāraṇyaka Upaniṣad (3.9.28), for example, *brahman* is described as awareness and bliss (*vijñānam ānandaṁ brahma*). In the same text (4.3.32), Yājñavalkya describes *brahman* as the highest bliss (*param ānandaḥ*). "On just a fraction of this bliss," he says, "do other creatures live."[26] While "bliss" is not an inappropriate rendering of *ānanda,* it is problematic and some clarification about its use is necessary.[27]

The principal problem arising from equating *ānanda* with bliss lies in the fact that bliss has its opposite condition, sorrow or unhappiness (*duḥkha*). Happiness and unhappiness are mutually exclusive and cannot simultaneously be present in the mind. Would this imply that the *ātman* is somehow supplanted whenever the mind is overcome by sorrow? Does the bliss of the *ātman* then manifest itself only when sorrowful mental states give way to conditions of happiness? The obvious difficulty with such an understanding is that it represents the *ātman* as limited by time since it implies that there is a mental state (viz., sorrow) when the *ātman* is absent. This would contradict the Upaniṣadic teaching that the *ātman* is timeless and present in all states and mental conditions. The understanding of *ānanda* as bliss also gives rise to the mistaken impression that the gain of the *ātman* results in an experience of happiness that is unlike any other.

If the translation of *ānanda* as "bliss" misleadingly equates the *ātman* with a transient mental conditon, what is a more appropriate rendering of this important term from the Upaniṣads? It is necessary to clarify that the term *ānanda,* as applied to *ātman,* refers to the very nature (*svarūpa*) of the *ātman* and not to an attribute or quality, since the *ātman* is free from all qualities (*nirguṇa*). As indicative of the nature of *ātman, ānanda* is better equated with limitlessness. It affirms that the *ātman* is free from the limits of time and space and, since it constitutes the essential nature of everything that exists, it is free also from the limitation of being an object among other objects.[28] It is synonymous therefore, with the term *anantam* (limitless) in the Taittirīya Upaniṣad's (2.1.1.) famous definition, *satyam jñānamanantam brahma.* All three terms, *satyam, jñānam,* and *anantam,* are not used as adjectives to distinguish *brahman* from a similar reality or realities, but to define the nature of *brahman.* The juxtaposition of *anantam* (limitless) with *satyam* (self-existent) and *jñānam* (self-evident) removes any suggestion of limits in the normal use of these terms.[29] In the popular Advaita formulation, *sat-cit-ānanda* the term "*cit*" is substituted for *jñānam* and *ānanda* for *ananta.* The self, as *ānanda,* is never an object of experience and present in all mental states (*vṛttis*), pleasant and unpleasant. The self-existent, self-revealing, and limitless *ātman* sustains all mental expressions. Any argument for the experience of *ānanda* as an object will contradict the non-duality of *brahman.* Texts defining *brahman* as *ānanda* must be understood as "setting forth the nature of Brahman and not signifying that the Bliss of the Self is cognized."[30]

With the clarification that *ānanda* points to the limitless (*ananta*) nature of the *ātman* and not to a changeful mental state, we may ask whether there is any value in the translation of *ānanda* as "bliss." The translation of *ānanda* as "bliss" is useful for emphasizing the desirability of *brahman* and the celebrative and joyful meaning of liberation. For the Advaita tradition, liberation (*mokṣa*), which is synonymous with the attainment of *brahman,* is not just the negation of sorrow (*duḥkha*), but the positive gain of bliss.[31] Knowing oneself to be nondifferent from the limitless (*ananta*) *brahman* engenders a state of contentment and fullness in one's mind that may be appropriately characterized as bliss (*ānanda*). It removes the misunderstanding of taking oneself to be mortal and unhappy.

The equation of *ānanda* with bliss also helps the Advaita tradition to refute the claim that the gain of the *ātman* leads to the attainment of a unique happiness, distinct and different from all other expressions of happiness. The

Advaita argument, to the contrary, is that all expressions of happiness reflect the nature (*svarūpa*) of the *ātman.* It is wrong, in other words, to conclude that there is an experience of happiness born out of contact between the senses and sense-objects or arising from the fulfillment of a desire that has its source in something other than the self. "Even worldy bliss," as Śaṅkara states it, "is a particle of the Bliss that is Brahman, which becomes transmuted into impermanent worldly bliss, consequent on knowledge becoming covered up by ignorance. . . ."[32]

Advaita supports the Upaniṣadic description of *brahman* as the sole source of bliss by drawing attention to the common human experience that there is no particular object that makes all people happy. An object that is desirable for one person may, at the same time, be a source of sorrow for another. The same object that is a source of joy for someone in the present may cease to be so in the future. Whether a person is happy or not with the gain of an object depends not so much on the object, but on its desirability. The Advaita claim is that in the fulfillment of a desire for a preferred object or goal, the mind of the desirer, hitherto agitated by desire, becomes desireless and free from agitation. At this time there is a condition of fullness that is identical with the nature of self. The person, however, does not understand this fullness to be identical with the limitless *ātman* and wrongly attributes it to the object or goal attained. The consequence is that the experience of happiness turns out, for various reasons, to be transient. Soon the mind grows tired or bored with its gain and seeks new objects for the attainment of happiness. These attainments bring, once more, momentary experiences of happiness, and the rollercoaster-like journey of life continues. The downhill thrill corresponds to the fleeting joy that one gains in the fulfillment of a desire. Then comes a lull when the mind yearns for a new gain. The uphill ride may be equated with the effort and struggle necessary for the satisfaction of the newly entertained desire. Even though *brahman,* as intrinsic bliss, is unchanging, experiential bliss seems to vary with the condition of one's mind. The all-pervading and intrinsic fullness constituting the nature of *brahman* thus appears to fluctuate.

> Again, according as ignorance and desire become attenuated, that very Bliss appears in the vision of one, who is learned, versed in the Vedas, and free from passion, as rising higher and higher a hundred-fold each time, in the planes starting with that of the man-Gandharvas, till the bliss of Hiraṇyagarbha is reached. But when the division of subject and object is eliminated by enlightenment, there is only the all-pervading and intrinsic Bliss that is one without a second.[33]

One who understands the nature of the self as limitless (*ananta*) is able to claim fullness without depending on the gain of anything outside the self to create the momentary state of freedom from want. Such a person, in the vision of the tradition, is liberated from desires that are rooted in self-ignorance and in the false idea that the source of fullness is something other than the self.

When a person, teaches Kṛṣṇa in Bhagavadgītā (2:55), gives up desires entertained by the mind, and is contented in the self, her wisdom is steady. Kṛṣṇa (2:70) compares the mind of such a person to the ocean that is always full. Its fullness does not increase with the flow of rivers into it and is not diminished if those rivers cease to flow. It knows itself to be the source of the water in all the rivers. *Brahman,* as *ānanda,* is desirable.

> Inasmuch as those Brāhmaṇas (who have realized Brahman) are seen to be as happy as one is from obtaining an external source of joy though, in fact, they do not take help of any external means of happiness, make no effort, and cherish no desires, it follows, as a matter of course, that Brahman is the source of their joy. Hence there does exist that Brahman which is full of joy, and is the spring of their happiness.[34]

Understanding that *brahman* is the source of all joy removes the misunderstanding that the knowledge of *brahman* leads to the gain of a special happiness that was never previously known. Advaita teaches that *brahman* is never outside human experience. As self-existent awareness, it is self-revealed, illumining and sustaining every thought and mental state, pleasant and unpleasant. The self-revealed nature of awareness however, does not resolve the problem of self-ignorance since one continues to confuse the self with the body and mind and one thinks of it as limited by time, space, and being an object among other objects. The reality of *brahman* in human experience does not eliminate ignorance about the nature of *brahman.* Experience has to be properly interpreted by a valid source of knowledge, and the Upaniṣads, in the view of Advaita, constitute such a valid source of knowledge.

THE *ĀTMAN* AS NON-DUAL

As the term *Advaita* (non-duality) suggests, the self is not two. I am currently typing this manuscript and I am aware of my body sitting on the floor of my study and of my fingers moving across keys of my computer. My body is an object of my awareness. I am also aware of my thoughts that vary as I move from idea to idea and try to clothe these in words that may be meaningful to a reader. As you read my words, you are aware of your body and of the thoughts generated in your mind in response to what you are reading. Our bodies and our minds differ, but the awareness that objectifies my body and mind and the awareness that objectifies your body and mind, claims Advaita, are identical. There are no differentiating qualities to distinguish awareness in one body from awareness in another. The one self, according to Advaita, is the self of all.

Using the terminology of the field (*kṣetra*) and the knower of the field (*kṣetrajña*), Kṛṣṇa, in Bhagavadgītā (13:33), uses a striking example to speak of the non-duality of the self and its nature as awareness. "As the sun alone," says Kṛṣṇa, "illumines this entire universe, so the Lord of the field illumines the entire field." As the one sun lights up our solar system, the one self illumines all bodies and all minds. The liberated person is described in the Bhagavdgītā (6:29) as seeing the self in all beings and all beings in the self. The consequence of this understanding, in the words of Īśa Upaniṣad (6), is that one is free from all hate.

The *ātman,* from the Advaita standpoint, is awareness, timeless, limitless, and identical in all beings. An object that originates in time, exists, and ceases to be, is limited by time. The limitation of time is referred to, in Sanskrit, as *kāla pariccheda.* The uncreated self that exists in all three periods of time without any loss of nature is obviously free from such time limitations. An object that exists within space, different from other objects, and which is not everywhere, is limited by space (*deśa pariccheda*). The identity of the self in everything, however, implies its transcendence of spatial limitations. The Upaniṣads repeatedly describe the self as all-pervasive. The pervasiveness of the self is not to be understood only in the sense that the self is within all things. The self is within all things and all things are within the self. Īśa Upaniṣad (5) describes the self as within the world and also outside of it. The knower of the self sees all beings in the self and the self in all beings.

Analogical arguments, supportive of the claims of the Upaniṣads about the *ātman,* are used by the Advaita tradition to demonstrate the reasonableness of these claims and to show that these do not contradict our knowledge of reality derived from other sources. I have used some of these arguments to discuss the nature of the self as timeless awareness. It is more difficult, however, to find analogical arguments to demonstrate and explain the all-pervasive nature of the self and its transcendence of spatial limitations. Swami Dayananda Saraswati uses the following argument to help the student appreciate the existence of all things in the self.

> Think of the moon. If I ask you the distance between the moon and yourself, you may reply that it is some definite number of miles. If I then ask, "What is the distance between space and the moon?" your answer will be that there cannot be any distance between the moon and space because the moon is in space and space is in and through the moon. Distance itself is the space between two objects in space, but between space and space there is no distance.
>
> Similarly, the sun, the sky, the stars all fall within Awareness. Your body falls within Awareness. Space falls within Awareness. There can be no distance. . . . You are Awareness, he is Awareness, she is Awareness, I am awareness. How many awarenesses are there? There is only one all-pervasive Awareness in which all objects exist.[35]

In a recent work, Peter Russell contends that the belief that awareness is located in the head is related to the location of the sense organs. Since our primary senses, eyes and ears, are located on our heads, the location for our experience of the world seems to be somewhere behind the eyes and between the ears. Russell asks us to imaginatively consider the transplantation of our eyes and ears to our knees and shifting the primary point of perception. "You would now be looking out onto the world from a different point and you might well imagine your consciousness to be in your knees. . . . Quite naturally, we place this image of the self at the center of our perceived world, giving us the sense of being *in* the world. But the truth is just the opposite: It is all within us."[36]

The popular Advaita story of the tenth person, which I cited at the beginning of this chapter, illustrates a significant loss through ignorance and a gain in the form of knowledge. The self, which is free from the limits of time and space and which is of the nature of limitless awareness, is misapprehended through ignorance. It is not differentiated from the body and mind and one considers oneself to be subject to birth and death and to be incomplete and wanting. Knowledge of the self, in Advaita, is not a process of becoming or the bringing into being of a new self. Advaita is a teaching tradition that aims at the removal of misconceptions about oneself and the engendering of correct knowledge. Misconception about the nature of the self is the primary cause of human sorrow, but incorrect assumptions about the self do not alter its nature. The self (*ātman*) is not different from the limitless (*brahman*) even when one erroneously takes it to be otherwise. Liberation is discovering and owning oneself to be what one already is: self-existent, limitless awareness.

In this chapter, many traditional Advaita pedagogical methods are employed to establish the nature of the *ātman* as awareness and to differentiate it from everything with which it is customarily and wrongly identified. These include the body, sense organs, and mind. In relation to the *ātman* (I), all of these are experienced as objects of knowledge and thus different from the *ātman*, the subject. The distinction between seer and seen (*dṛg-dṛṣya prakriyā*) is used to point to the *ātman* as nonobjectifiable, illuminating awareness. Although such methods of teaching are necessary for distinguishing the self from the non-self, these must be properly understood as early steps in a teaching process. If the teaching ends here, even with the claim that the self is identical in all, the result is a duality consisting of self and non-self.

Advaita (non-duality) is established not only through a teaching about the sameness of the self in all (*sarvabhūtastham ātmānaṁ*), but ultimately by the understanding that the *ātman*, which is identical with *brahman*, constitutes the essential nature of all that exists.[37] Non-duality is affirmed by a denial of ontological plurality through the argument that effects are essentially non-different from their cause. The teaching method of Advaita involves drawing attention to the *ātman* as self-illumining awareness, its identity with *brahman*, and the nature of the world as non-separate from *brahman*. The Upaniṣads present *brahman* as both the intelligent and material cause (*nimitta upādāna kāraṇa*) of the world which is its effect (*kārya*). As an effect, the world is non-separate from, dependent on, and partakes of the nature of *brahman*, even as clay pots partake of the nature of clay. *Brahman*, however, is independent and does not partake of the nature of the world. The world is non-different from *brahman,* but *brahman* is not identical with the world. The world, in other words, does not have any ontological reality or existence independent of *brahman.* The body, mind, and senses are only initially set apart from *brahman.* These belong to the world and must also be understood to be ontologically non-separate from *brahman. Brahman* constitutes the single reality (*satyam*) of everything.

CHAPTER FOUR

The Source of Valid Knowledge

In chapter 3 we discussed the Advaita understanding of the nature of the self (*ātman*). The *ātman* is self-existent awareness, limitless and non-dual. The self (*ātman*), in other words, is non-different from the infinite (*brahman*). The purpose of Advaita is to teach this identity between *ātman* and *brahman* as proclaimed in the great sentences (*mahāvakyas*) of the Upaniṣads and, in particular, in the Chāndogya Upaniṣad (6.8.7) instruction, "That Thou Art" (*tat tvam asi*). These claims about the nature of the self are different from the assumptions that are commonly held. The self is generally equated with the body and mind complex and believed to be subject to all the characteristics of these such as birth and death. It is thought to be incomplete and different in each being. What is the source of these extraordinary Advaita claims about the nature of the self? What is the traditional Advaita self-understanding regarding the authority for its view of the self?[1]

THE SIGNIFICANCE OF A VALID MEANS OF KNOWLEDGE

The Sanskrit word *pramā* is used to denote knowledge that is valid, and the source of any valid knowledge is termed a *pramāṇa*. A *pramāṇa*, therefore, is defined by Advaita as the cause of valid knowledge (*pramā karaṇam pramāṇam*).[2] In the view of Śaṅkara, knowledge is produced only by a valid means of knowledge and the claims of any source must be evaluated by its ability to do so.[3]

> A means of knowledge is or is not such according as it leads or does not lead to valid knowledge. Otherwise even a post, for instance, would be considered a means of knowledge in perceiving sound etc.[4]

Śaṅkara does not express any doubts or reservations about the ability of the *pramāṇas* to generate knowledge in their respective spheres. He claims, in fact, that the day to day affairs of the world will become impossible if the *pramāṇas* are considered to be unreliable. People who have experienced that hunger and thirst are satisfied by eating and drinking infer that the continued use of these means will produce similar results. If such inferences are doubted, argues Śaṅkara, eating and drinking will not be possible.[5]

THE LIMITS OF PERCEPTION AND INFERENCE

Which source of valid knowledge (*pramāṇa*) is appropriate for knowing *brahman,* which is non-different from the self (*ātman*)? Throughout his commentaries, Śaṅkara explains why sense perception (*pratyakṣa*) is not an appropriate means for knowing *brahman.* Each of the five sense organs is capable of revealing a quality that is unique to its own nature. Forms, sounds, taste, scent, and sensation are the qualities known through the senses. Although *brahman* is an ever-existing entity, it cannot be known through the senses because it possesses none of these qualities. It is without form, sound, taste, scent, and sensation. In the words of Kaṭha Upaniṣad (3:15):

> It has no sound or touch,
> no appearance, taste, or smell;
> It is without beginning or end,
> undecaying and eternal;
> When a man perceives it,
> fixed and beyond the immense,
> He is freed from the jaws of death.

Brahman is limitless and non-dual awareness; to be the object of a sense organ is to be finite and delimited. A *brahman* that can be known through the senses is a contradiction. However magnified one may imagine the capacity of the senses to be, these are still an inappropriate *pramāṇa* for knowing *brahman.*

Along with the limits of the sense organs, there is also the impossibility of objectifying *brahman,* the limitless. Perceptual knowledge involves a process of objectification or knowing by making things the objects of our knowledge. By the act of objectification, the things that we wish to know become available for examination and analysis. *Brahman,* as we have seen in chapter 3, is awareness, the illuminator of the body, senses, and the mind. It is the constant subject and its objectification would require the existence of another self, which does not exist. As Śaṅkara puts it in his Kena Upaniṣad (2.1) commentary, "The knower cannot be known by the knower, just as fire cannot be consumed by the consuming fire; and there is no other knower different from *brahman* to whom *brahman* can become a separate knowable."

If perception is unsuitable as a means of knowledge for *brahman,* then so also are those sources that depend upon data gathered through perception. These include inference, comparison, postulation, and noncognition. Inferential knowledge is based on the invariable relationship between the thing inferred (*sādhya*) and the ground from which the inference is made (*hetu*).

Brahman, however, has no apprehensible quality with which it is invariably related and which can serve as the ground of an inference. Its existence, therefore, cannot be established by inference.

> As for the argument that *brahman* being an existing thing, other means of knowledge should apply to It, that too is a mere figment of the brain. For this Entity is not an object of perception, It being devoid of all grounds of inference etc. But like the religious acts (producing virtue), this entity is known from the scriptures alone.[6]

One cannot ascertain the nature of *brahman* through any form of reasoning that operates independently of a valid source of knowledge. Such reasoning, in the view of Śaṅkara, is at best conjectural in nature and cannot establish anything conclusively. While Śaṅkara does not deny the value of human reasoning, he is clear about its limits as a valid means for the knowledge of *brahman.* "Although reasoning may be noticed to have finality in some, still in the present context it cannot possibly get immunity from the charge of being inconclusive; for this extremely sublime subject matter, concerned with the reality of the cause of the universe and leading to the goal of liberation, cannot even be guessed without the help of the Vedas. And we said that It cannot be known either through perception, being devoid of form etc., or through inference, etc., being devoid of grounds of inference."[7] Śaṅkara is supportive of reasoning processes that are in harmony with the revelation of the Vedas and which generate support for these teachings.

THE VEDAS AS THE MEANS OF KNOWLEDGE FOR *BRAHMAN*

As the quotation above from Śaṅkara suggests, the Vedas, in his view, are the appropriate and authoritative source for the knowledge of *brahman.* In addition to *brahman,* the Vedas, for Advaita, also serve as a valid source for the knowledge of *dharma,* which includes right ethical and ritual conduct and their respective results. The Vedas are the source of our knowledge about actions that produce subtle meritorious results (*puṇya*) and those which produce subtle unmeritorious consequences (*pāpa*). *Puṇya* results in future happiness while *pāpa* produces pain. The Vedas enjoin us to choose actions that produce the former and avoid the latter. While the necessity and value of certain ethical choices, such as telling the truth or not stealing, may be established by observation and reason, their connection to future happiness, especially in another life, cannot be so demonstrated. One must accept the existence of the self in a future life in order to be motivated to avoid pain and attain happiness in that life. The knowledge of the existence of the self in a future body is revealed in the Vedas.[8] It is from the Vedas also that we learn of obligatory duties such as the necessity to perform daily at dawn, noon, and dusk the ritual of *sandhyāvandanam* or the annual *śrāddha* ceremony on behalf of one's departed ancestors. The Vedas also reveal various optional rituals (*kamya karmas*), such as the *jyotiṣṭoma* for the attainment of heaven or the *putrakāmeṣṭi* for the birth of a child. The nonperformance of obligatory rituals brings demerit (*pāpa*) while the performance of optional ones leads to the accrual of merit (*puṇya*).

In the view of Śaṅkara, the revelation of *dharma* is the authoritative concern of the first three sections of the Vedas (the *Samhitās, Brāhmaṇas,* and *Āraṇyakas*) referred to collectively as the *karmakāṇḍa* (ritual section). These sections of the Vedas are concerned with providing scripturally approved methods for the attainment of wealth, power, and fame (*artha*) and pleasure (*kāma*) here and in the hereafter. The *karmakāṇḍa* specifies the proper ethical and ritual action, encompassed in the word *dharma,* for the accomplishment of these ends.

Pūrva Mīmāṁsā, an ancient tradition of Vedic exegesis, holds the view that the Vedas are an authoritative revelation, but only for *dharma.* For this school of thought, only the injunctions (*vidhi*) enjoining the performance of acceptable actions and prohibitions (*niṣedha*) forbidding actions that are opposed to *dharma* are authoritative. All other parts of the Vedas are secondary and dependent for their significance and meaning on a connection with the injunctions. The final section of the Vedas, the Upaniṣads, are viewed by Pūrva Mīmāṁsā as an appendage to the injunctive texts which either praise these texts or provide information that is useful for the performance of Vedic rituals. The Upaniṣads, it is claimed, do not have any independent subject matter.[9]

For Śaṅkara and the Advaita tradition, on the other hand, the Vedas are an authoritative source of knowledge for both *dharma* and *brahman. Dharma* is the subject matter of the first three sections of the Vedas, while *brahman* is the subject matter of the fourth section, the Upaniṣads, referred to as the *jñānakāṇḍa* (knowledge section).[10] If the qualified student for the ritual section is the one who is desirous of pleasure in this or other worlds, the qualified student for the knowledge section is the one who has discovered the limits of pleasure by reflecting deeply on the nature of her experiences in the world and has developed an attitude of detachment in relation to these. She possesses what we referred to in chapter 2 as *viveka* (the capacity to distinguish the timeless from the timebound) and *vairāgya* (freedom from longing for objects of pleasure in this or other worlds). The two sections of the Vedas, therefore, differ in respect to (1) subject matter (*viṣaya*), (2) qualified student (*adhikārī*), and (3) result (*phala*). The *karmakāṇḍa* has pleasure as its result, while the result of the *jñānakāṇḍa* is liberation (*mokṣa*).

KNOWLEDGE AND THE ATTAINMENT OF *BRAHMAN*

There is a fourth difference between the ritual section and the knowledge sections of the Vedas that is central to Śaṅkara's understanding of the latter as a source for knowing *brahman.* The ritual section of the Vedas, as we have noted above, provides information about rites that lead to desirable results such as the heavenly world or the birth of a child. It also provides information about which actions are meritorious and produce pleasurable future effects and which actions are to be avoided because of their potentially unpleasant results. The information revealed in the first section of the Vedas is not an end in itself. The details of the ritual for the birth of a child, for example, are not useful until the actual ritual is performed. To ensure the birth of a child, the knowledge of the ritual must be followed by its implementation. The same holds true for ethical actions. The mere knowledge of what constitutes a proper action does not produce subtle positive effects (*puṇya*). Again, a choice has to be exercised in action for the attainment of the desired result. The reason for this is that the end to be accomplished does not already exist. It has to be brought into existence through the application of knowledge in action. Since the object to be attained is not yet in existence, the relationship between the words of the ritual section and this object is an indirect one. Words alone do not lead to the gain of the object.

In the view of Śaṅkara, the words of the Upaniṣads, which constitute the knowedge section of the Vedas (*jñānakāṇḍa*), are the valid means (*pramāṇa*) for the knowledge of *brahman*. What is the relationship between the words of the Upaniṣads and the self (*ātman*) which is identical with *brahman*? Is the relationship also an indirect one? Are words only capable of producing indirect knowledge (*parokṣa jñānam*) or can words, in certain circumstances, produce direct knowledge (*aparokṣa jñānam*)?[11] Let us return for a moment to the story of the tenth person in chapter 3. When the woodcutter said to the leader, "You are the tenth person," the result was immediate. The "'lost" person was, at that moment itself, "found." The words of the woodcutter, by themselves, "produced" the desired result—the tenth person. Knowledge was direct and the results were immediate.

The words of the woodcutter were able to produce direct and immediate results because the end to be attained (viz., the tenth person) was already in existence and available right there. He was never separate from the group by time or space. The problem that confronted the disciples was one of ignorance (*avidyā*) about someone who was never, in reality, lost. The "finding" of the tenth person was not the bringing into being of one who was hitherto nonexistent. It was the discovery of an immediately available person, mistakenly thought to be drowned. A solution of this kind is described in Advaita to be one of "gaining that which is already gained" referred to, in Sanskrit, as *prāptasya prāpti*. It is distinguished from "gaining that which is not yet gained" or *aprāptasya prāpti*. Where the problem is one of *prāptasya prāpti*, words can serve as a direct means of knowledge and bring forth an immediate result. It is clear that Śaṅkara understands the gain of *brahman* to be a solution of this kind and hence his claim for the validity of the words of the Upaniṣads.

THE SELF-REVEALING NATURE OF *BRAHMAN*

In his commentary on the *Brahmasūtra*, Śaṅkara has an objector asking whether *brahman* is known or unknown.[12] The point of the objector's inquiry is that if *brahman* is known, a case cannot be made for the Upaniṣads as a valid means of knowledge for *brahman.* The texts become redundant. If, on the other hand, *brahman* is entirely unknown, it cannot become the object of any kind of inquiry. Śaṅkara, in his reply, denies that *brahman* is entirely unknown. "The existence of *brahman,*" claims Śaṅkara, "is well known from the fact of Its being the Self of all; for everyone feels that his Self exists, and he never feels 'I do not exist.' Had there been no general recognition of the existence of the Self, everyone would have felt, 'I do not exist.' And the Self is *Brahman.*"

As awareness, the self is self-revealing. It shines of itself and does not require the assistance of anything to make its existence known. As the Kaṭha Upaniṣad (5:15) poetically states it, it is in the light of the self that everything else shines.

> There the sun does not shine,
> nor the moon and stars;
> There lightning does not shine.
> of this common fire we need not speak!
> Him alone, as he shines, do all things reflect:
> this whole world radiates with his light.

The *ātman* is the content of the word *I* and it is because of its self-revealing nature that one has the immediate sense of existing. A person cannot question his or her existence without, at the same time, proclaiming it. To say, "I do not exist," means, "I am aware that I do not exist." The existence of the self, as awareness, is implied in this statement. The words of the Upaniṣads do not reveal an entirely unknown self. The self-revealing or self-luminous nature of the *ātman* is an argument to which Śaṅkara repeatedly returns. The existence of objects needs to be established by proper means of knowledge, but the same is not true for the self. This is such an important issue in understanding the significance of the *śruti* in Śaṅkara that one of his lengthy expositions on the self-revealing and self-luminous nature of the *ātman* is worth citing in full.

> Any idea of the possibility of denying the existence of the Self is illogical, just because it is the Self. For the Self of any one does not require to be revealed to any one with the help of any other means. For such means of knowledge as perception etc., that are taken up for proving the existence of other things that remain unknown, belong to this very Self. Not that space and other things are understood by anyone to be self-established, independently of other means of knowledge. But the self being the basis of all such empirical dealings as the use of the means of knowledge, stands there as a postulate even prior to the use of those means. And it is not possible to deny such a Self; for it is an adventitious thing alone that can be repudiated, but not so one's own nature. The Self constitutes the very nature of the man who would deny it. The heat of fire cannot be denied by the fire itself.[13]

IGNORANCE AS INCOMPLETE KNOWLEDGE OF *BRAHMAN*

If the self, as Śaṅkara insists, reveals itself and is the content of the "I" thought, what is the need then for a means of knowledge to know the self? The problem, argues Śaṅkara, is that while the self as awareness shines of itself in the mind, and one knows oneself to be an existent being, the specific nature of the self remains unknown. It is generally identified with the I-thought or ego and not appreciated as its ground (*adhiṣṭhāna*) and witness.

> Leaving aside the (erroneous) knowledge of the Self as the agent (of actions) as contained in the idea of "I," the (real) Self—which is the witness of the idea of "I," which exists in all creatures, which is without any difference of degrees, and which is one, unchanging, eternal and all-pervasive consciousness—(such a Self) is not known as the Self of all by anyone in the section of the Vedas dealing with virtuous deeds or in the scriptures of logicians.[14]

One has a generalized knowledge (*sāmānya jñāna*) of the self, but does not understand its essential nature (*viśeṣa jñāna*) as identical with the limitless *brahman* that is communicated through the words of the Upaniṣads. It is, in fact, the lack of specific knowledge of the self that enables a person to incorrectly identify the self with the body, mind, and senses and regard it to be subject to the limits and deficiencies of these. If the self is entirely unknown, it cannot be erroneously taken, as it usually is, for something else. Self-ignorance therefore, as understood by Śaṅkara, is not the complete absence of knowledge about the self. It is the incomplete knowledge of the self that causes its misapprehension. The self, as the content of the "I" thought, is immediately available, since a person is never separate from herself in time or space and possesses an indubitable sense of existence. The self, like the tenth person, does not have to be created. The task of the teacher, with the help of the Upaniṣads, is to remove misunderstandings about the distinctive nature of the self and lead the student to appreciate the self's identity with *brahman*, which is of the nature of limitless awareness.

It is important to remember that misunderstanding about the self does not bring about any change in the nature of the self. Thinking that the self is subject to birth and death, or that it ages and changes with the body, does not cause the self to become so. Similarly, thinking that one is unhappy and insufficient does not diminish the nature of the self as being full and without limits. If erroneous conclusions about the nature of the self do not alter its nature, correct knowledge does not also bring about any change in the self. Knowledge gained from the Upaniṣads simply reveals the self to be what it has always been.

The problem of self-ignorance, therefore, is not one of complete ignorance about oneself. It is one of misunderstanding the nature of the self that is immediately available and manifesting unceasingly as self-existent awareness.

For a problem of this kind, the words of the Upaniṣads can be an immediate and adequate solution. It is in this context that one must understand Śaṅkara's refutation of action (*karman*) as a direct means for the attainment of the self.[15] Action, in the view of Śaṅkara, is a direct means where one strives to gain something that is not yet gained (*aprāptasya prāpti*), and such actions are of four kinds: creating, modifying, reaching, and purifying. *Brahman* cannot be the object of an act of creation or modification since it is an already existing being and its essential nature is beyond all transformation. If *brahman* is a created entity, liberation, which is the attainment of *brahman,* will be transient since, as Śaṅkara puts it, "it is a matter of common experience that anything that is produced by action is impermanent. Should liberation be the result of action it would be transitory."[16]

Since *brahman* is the self and not separate from anyone or anything by time or space, there is no question of the need for an action to reach *brahman.* "*Brahman* is all-pervasive and non-different from the goers. *Brahman* is omnipresent because it is the (material) cause of *ākāśa* (space) etc., and all conscious souls are non-different from *brahman.* Hence, liberation is not (an) achievable (result). A traveler has to reach a place which is different from himself. Not that the very place which is non-different from oneself can be reached by oneself."[17] And acts of purification are not necessary in the case of *brahman,* which is pure and free from all blemish and cannot be the object of any kind of action.

> The attainment of the self cannot be, as in the case of things other than it, the obtaining of something not obtained before, for here there is no difference between the person attaining and the object attained. Where the self has to obtain something other than itself, the self is the attainer and the non-self is the object attained. This, not being already attained, is separated by acts such as producing and is to be attained by the initiation of a particular action with the help of auxiliaries. . . . But this self is the very opposite of that. By the very fact of its being the self, it is not separate by acts such as producing. But although it is always attained, it is separated by ignorance only.[18]

KNOWLEDGE AND EXPERIENCE

The *ātman,* as Śaṅkara explains, is not entirely unknown and ignorance is a problem of misapprehension and not the complete absence of knowledge. This incomplete knowledge, in fact, becomes the basis for instruction about *brahman,* since it is impossible to instruct about something that is completely unknown. *Brahman,* as we noted in chapter 3, is *ānanda* and all forms of happiness are expressions of *brahman.*[19] Similarly, it is because of the self-revealing nature of *brahman* that all possess an indubitable sense of existence. *Brahman* shines in the mind as existence that is the content of the thought, "I am." Yet, in spite of knowing happiness and the immediate sense of one's existence, one is still ignorant of *brahman.* The experience of *brahman* as happiness or existence in the mind is clearly not the same as the knowledge of *brahman* since experience, as is the case here, is misconstrued. Although *brahman* is experienced as happiness, the source of this happiness is usually attributed to some external object. Similarly, while *brahman* is the explanation for knowing that one exists, this existence is identified with the body and the limitless self-evident nature of *brahman* remains unknown. Experience, therefore, by itself, is not identical with valid knowledge and often needs to be correctly interpreted by an appropriate source of knowledge. The role of the Upaniṣads, in relation to the presence of *brahman* as happiness and existence, is to correct our misunderstanding and to identify these with the very nature of *brahman.*

While experience may or may not coincide with valid knowledge, valid knowledge does have an experiential dimension. The knowledge of *brahman,* gained from the words of the Upaniṣads, is experiential in the sense that the mental and emotional disposition of a person who knows herself to be *brahman* is different from that of someone who lacks this knowledge.[20] Śaṅkara himself continuously points to the inward state of the knower of *brahman* as evidence of the efficacy of the words of the Upaniṣads. "Do you not see," asks Śaṅkara, "the result of knowledge in the removal of evils which are the root of transmigration, such as ignorance, grief, delusion, and fear? Or do you not hear those hundreds of Upaniṣadic texts such as 'Then what delusion and what grief can there be for one who sees unity'?" (IS 7).[21] The knower of *brahman* is repeatedly described in the Upaniṣads as being free from sorrow, hate, grief, greed, and fear. Positively, the knowledge of *brahman* is synonymous with the attainment of peace and abiding happiness. While this transformation is clearly experiential in nature, it is the fruit of right knowledge ascertained through inquiry into the appropriate *pramāṇa.* Knowledge gives rise to emotional and mental experiences that reflect and are consistent with the nature of the self, but such states of mind do not constitute an independent source of knowledge for the self.

Brahman is always within the range of human experience as awareness and as happiness. Such experience, however, is compatible with ignorance about the self's nature since awareness is erroneously identified with the body, senses, and mind, and happiness is attributed to objects other than the self. As a consequence of instruction from the Upaniṣad, the meaning of experience is reinterpreted and existence and happiness are identified with the nature of *brahman.* Experience and knowledge, in other words, now coincide.[22]

THE DILEMMA OF KNOWING THE KNOWER

The Upaniṣads are the means of knowledge for *brahman,* and the texts consist of words. *Brahman,* however, is not one object among other objects in space and time and cannot be known in the manner of sense objects. It is not available for observation and analysis through objectification. It is important to remember also that *brahman* is not available for objectification and scrutiny within the mind. *Brahman* is the awareness that illumines all thoughts and emotions. To observe *brahman* as an object in one's mind would require another illumining awareness. Further, awareness cannot be bifurcated into both subject and object in the mind. Kena Upaniṣad (4) expresses this truth poetically in the claim that the self is that which "one cannot grasp with one's mind, by which, they say, the mind itself is grasped." In the Bṛhadāraṇyaka Upaniṣad (3.4.1) the teacher, Yājñavalkya, explaining the nature of the self as a non-object of the mind and senses to his student, Uṣasta Cākrāyaṇa, teaches that one "can't see the seer who does the seeing; you can't hear the hearer who does the hearing; you can't think of the thinker who does the thinking; and you can't perceive the perceiver who does the perceiving. The self within all is this self of yours. All else besides this is grief!"

In spite of numerous texts like this, Śaṅkara is never skeptical about the possibility of knowing *brahman* through the Upaniṣads. To the argument that it is contradictory for the scriptures to describe *brahman* as unknowable and also known, Śaṅkara explains that such texts deny that the self, "like other things, is known by any other means than scriptural evidence. Other things are cognized by ordinary means independent of scriptural evidence; but the truth of the self cannot be known by any other means of knowledge but that."[23] Śaṅkara generally interprets Upaniṣad texts that speak of the unknowability of *brahman* in two ways. He interprets some of these texts as refuting the possibility of knowing *brahman* as an object, while others are seen as emphasizing the exclusivity of the Upaniṣads as the valid means of knowledge.[24]

Śaṅkara maintains throughout that the words of the Upaniṣads (*Vedānta vākyas*) are the valid means of knowledge for *brahman* and that the instrument of knowledge is the mind.[25] Bṛhadāraṇyaka Upaniṣad (4.4.19) says that the self is to be known through the mind alone (*manasaivānudrṣṭavyam*), and Śaṅkara explains that the mind, "purified by the knowledge of the supreme truth, and in accordance with the instructions of the teacher," is the instrument of knowledge. In his commentary on the Bhagavadgītā, Śaṅkara explains that the mind, "refined by *śama* and *dama*—i.e., by the subjugation of the body, the mind and senses—and equipped with the teachings of the scripture and the teacher, constitutes the sense by which the self may be seen."[26]

The proposition of the mind as the instrument through which the self can be known leads to a significant dilemma. The process of empirical knowledge involves a distinction between the subject and object, the knower and known. We know things by making these the objects of our awareness and, in this way, they become available for our scrutiny and analysis. Knowledge of an object presupposes the subject, the knower. *Brahman,* however, is the eternal subject. As awareness, it illumines everything and the entire universe, including mind, body, and senses, is its object. It is impossible for illumining awareness to be made an object of knowledge. It is not possible for the subject to be conceived as an object since, in its absence, there is no subject to know the subject as an object. Śaṅkara, commenting on Bṛhadāraṇyaka Upaniṣad 2.4.14, puts the problem succinctly:

> The knower may desire to know, not about itself, but about objects. As fire does not burn itself, so the self does not know itself, and the knower can have no knowledge of a thing that is not its object. Therefore through what instrument should one know the knower owing to which this universe is known and who should know it? And when to the knower of *brahman* who has discriminated the Real from the unreal there remains only the subject, absolute and one without a second, *through what instrument O Maitreyī should one know that Knower?*

How could knowledge of *brahman* occur in the mind without the suggestion that *brahman* becomes a mental object?

In suggesting a resolution to what appear to be contradictory Advaita claims, the impossibility of objectifying *brahman* and the insistence that it must be known in the mind, we must return to Śaṅkara's understanding of the nature of valid knowledge. On of his clearest comments on this issue occurs in his commentary on *Brahmasūtra* 1.1.2 (*janmādyasya yataḥ*) where he is differentiating between action, worldly and religious, and knowledge. Actions, according to Śaṅkara, offer scope for human choice in the sense that alternative ways of doing something may be possible. Knowledge, on the other hand, is dependent on the nature of the object to be known and offers no scope for alternative human choices. Valid knowledge, in other words, corresponds to the nature of the object that one is desirous of knowing. As Śaṅkara puts it, "An awareness of the form, 'This is a stump, or a man, or something else,' with regard to the same stump cannot be valid knowledge. In such a case, the awareness of the form, 'This is a man or something else' is erroneous, but 'This is a stump to be sure' is valid knowledge; for it corresponds to the thing itself. Thus the validity of the knowledge of an existing thing is determined by the thing itself."[27]

Valid knowledge is knowledge that corresponds to the nature of the object one is desirous of knowing. This occurs when the thought form (*antaḥkaraṇa vṛtti*) occurring in the mind is true to the object apprehended. If, for example, I am walking along the street when it is dark and I perceive an object that happens to be a rope lying in my way and I mistake it for a snake with the thought, "This is a snake," my knowledge is obviously false. The thought form, "This is a snake," does not correspond with the nature of the object, a rope. When the object does not move and I approach closely, I discover it to be a rope. There is a corresponding change in my mind, "This is a rope," which constitutes valid knowledge. In the latter case, there is correspondence between the thought form and the external object.

In the case of the *ātman,* ignorance takes the form of erroneous thought forms that misconstrue the nature of the ever-present and luminous self and identify it with the body, mind, senses, etc. Ignorance involves superimposition (*adhyāsa*) of attributes belonging to the object (body, sense, mind) on the subject, the self, and vice versa.[28]

> One superimposes the characteristics of the body when one has such ideas as "I am fat," "I am thin," "I am fair. . . ." So also one superimposes the attributes of the senses and organs when one thinks, "I am dumb," "I have lost one eye." "I am a eunuch," "I am deaf. . . ." Similarly, one superimposes the attributes of the internal organ, such as desire, will, doubt, perseverance, etc. In the same way, one first superimposes the internal organ, possessed of the idea of ego on the self, the witness of all the manifestations of that organ; then by an opposite process, one superimposes on the internal organ etc. that self which is opposed to the non-self and which is the witness of everything.[29]

Incorrect assertions about the nature of the self must give way to valid assertions, corresponding to the nature of the self and derived from the Upaniṣads. The mind is the locus of error, and right knowledge is a process occurring within the mind and not transcending it.

For this process to occur, a special disposition of mind is necessary and the qualifications of discipleship, discussed in chapter 2, are meant for making the mind a suitable instrument for the knowledge of the self. Śaṅkara's emphasis on the proper disposition of mind must be seen in relation to the uniqueness of *brahmajñāna.* Knowledge is generally concerned with objects other than oneself. When I recognize the tree outside my window to be an apple tree, the thought form that accompanies this recognition is not centered on the self. The self, as awareness, illumines this apple tree thought as well as the condition of my mind in which this thought occurs. If I am agitated when I recognize the apple tree, awareness reveals my agitated mind and the apple tree thought. If I am angry or envious of someone when I perceive the apple tree, such states will also be revealed. A special disposition of the mind, engendered through the cultivation of the qualities of discipleship, is not necessary for my knowledge of the apple tree. In the case of the self, however, appropriate thought forms as well as clarity and calmness of mind are necessary. The aim of knowledge is to distinguish the self from everything that is not-self and with which the self is wrongly identified. In a distracted and outwardly directed mind, the presence of the self as illumining awareness cannot be appreciated. Negative states of mind such as greed, anger, hate, and envy cause mental unrest, reinforce confusion between the self and non-self and direct attention away from the ever-present self. These must, therefore, be controlled and sublimated by cultivating and practicing the fourfold means.

Let us illustrate this point with the help of an analogy. Imagine three buckets of water, one muddy, one turbulent, and the other still and clear. In all three buckets, the sun shines equally. If one desires a reflection of the sun that is faithful to the sun's nature, such a reflection will not be possible in the muddy and agitated buckets. In one, the sun appears dull and, in the other, it appears to be in motion. The image is difficult to distinguish from the reflecting medium.

In the still and clear bucket, however, the sun is reflected in its brilliant and motionless nature. Similarly, a clear and still mind becomes a necessary instrument for appreciating the self as awareness that is not to be identified with any specific mental state.[30] Commenting on Muṇḍaka Upaniṣad, Śaṅkara proffers one of his clearest statements on mental purity (*viśuddhasattva*).

> Though the intellect in all beings is intrinsically able to make the self known, still, being polluted by such blemishes as attachment to external objects etc., it becomes agitated and impure, and does not, like a stained mirror or ruffled water, make the reality of the self known, though it is ever at hand. The favourableness of the intellect comes about when it continues to be transparent and tranquil on having been made clean like a mirror, water etc., by the removal of the pollution caused by the dirt of attachment, springing from the contact of the sense and the sense-objects.[31]

While a translucent and pure mind, referred to as *sattvaśuddhi,* is necessary for the gain of self-knowledge, it is important to emphasize that this mental condition is not a direct cause of self-knowledge. An impure and agitated mind is subject to ignorance (*avidyā*), but so also is a pure and still mind. The difference is that the latter mind enjoys a disposition that is favorable to the gain of knowledge. In his commentary on the Bhagavadgītā, Śaṅkara explains that virtues such as humility, etc., are conducive to the gain of knowledge and are to be regarded as secondary or auxiliary causes.[32] These virtues themselves do not constitute a valid means of knowledge and their cultivation does not make the Upaniṣads redundant. The mind that is tranquil still needs knowledge about the nature of the self, arising from the words of the Upaniṣads. Śaṅkara mentions the necessity for instruction, side by side with his emphasis on mental preparation. Knowledge of the self, says Śaṅkara, is unattainable by those who have not been properly initiated into the traditional knowledge by the teachers, who have not studied the teachings of the Vedānta, whose intellect dwells in the realms of the senses, and who have not been trained in the right sources of knowledge.[33] Positively, self-knowledge occurs through the favorable disposition of the mind and the instruction of the teacher and scripture. Commenting on Kaṭha Upaniṣad (2.1.11), "This is to be attained through the mind (*manasaivedamāptavyam*)," Śaṅkara interprets the sentence to indicate the mind that has been purified by the teacher and the scriptures.[34]

In a calm and translucent mind, invalid thought forms about the nature of *brahman* are replaced by valid thought forms, generated by the teachings of the *guru* and the scripture, which coincide with the nature of *brahman.*[35] The essence of such valid knowledge is, "I am awareness, unlimited by time and space, full and complete."[36] These are thought forms, unlike previous ones, that do not contradict the nature of the self or objectify it. It is these thought forms that destroy ignorance. In the placid lake of the mind, the self recognizes itself, not as an object, but as awareness, the ever-present subject.

Kena Upaniṣad illustrates the challenges of language in describing *brahman* and transmitting the knowledge of *brahman.* The challenge is to affirm the reality of knowing *brahman,* without suggesting that it is an object. The teacher (1.4) speaks of *brahman* as different from the known and unknown. Commenting on this statement, Śaṅkara explains that *brahman* is to be distinguished from things that are known, since objects of knowledge are limited and finite. By describing *brahman* as different from the unknown, the teacher wants to make the point that it is not a thing to be obtained and that it is one's own self. "Thus the statement that *brahman* is different from the known and unknown, having amounted to *brahman* being denied as an object to be acquired or rejected, the desire of the disciple to know *brahman* (objectively) comes to an end, for *brahman* is non-different from the self. For nothing other than one's own self can possibly be different from the known and the unknown."[37]

Clarifying that the knowledge of *brahman* is gained through appropriate thought-forms does not entirely explain how the knower is known. Another step is necessary, and this requires identifying the recipient of instruction. The self, as awareness, simply is. From its own standpoint, it is characterized neither by ignorance or knowledge, both of which are meaningful terms only with reference to the mind. The self illumines knowledge as well as ignorance. As Śaṅkara puts it in BUBh 4.4.6, "there is no such distinction as liberation and bondage in the self, for it is eternally the same; but the ignorance regarding it is removed by the knowledge arising from the teachings of the scriptures, and prior to the receiving of these teachings, the effort to attain liberation is perfectly reasonable." Ignorance is not a condition of the self, but of the ego, or I-notion, which is also a thought. In his commentary on BU 4.4.6, Śaṅkara responds to an objector's argument that the self is subject to ignorance since one sometimes has the sense of being confused or not knowing. Śaṅkara rejects this conclusion on the basis that ignorance is an object witnessed by the self. Something that is experienced as an object cannot be an integral part of the subject.

> You say that a person feels, "I do not know, I am confused"; thereby you admit that he visualizes his ignorance and confusion, in other words, that these become the objects of his experience. So how can the ignorance and confusion, which are objects, be at the same time a description of the subject, the perceiver? If, on the other hand, they are a description of the subject, how can they be objects and be perceived by the subject? An object is perceived by an act of the subject. The object is one thing, and the subject another; it cannot be perceived by itself. Tell me how under such circumstances the ignorance and confusion can be a description of the subject. Moreover, a person who sees ignorance as something distinct—perceives it as an object of his own cognition—does not regard it as an attribute of the perceiver, as is the case with thinness, colour, and so forth in the body.[38]

In Sanskrit, this I-notion is referred to as the *ahamvṛtti* (I-thought), or the *ahaṁkāra.* The I-thought is the thinker, feeler, enjoyer, doer, and experiencer. It comes into being as a consequence of the presence of awareness in the mind. Ignorance is not a problem for the physical body that is inert. The self, as awareness, does not commit the error of taking itself to be anything. Ignorance is a problem for the ego or I-thought which confuses the self (*ātman*) and non-self (*anātman*). Whereas other thoughts come and go because the objects on which they are centered are impermanent and occupy the attention of the ego for a limited time span, the I-thought enjoys a relative permanency. This permanency is the consequence of the fact that the I-thought is centered on an awareness that is permanently present, being timeless and self-revealing. Its content and nature are nothing but awareness, without which it has no existence or reality. When the I-thought, whose nature is limitless awareness, non-different from *brahman,* is subject to ignorance, it identifies itself with the characteristics of the body, senses, and mind in notions such as, "I am short," "I am blind," or "I am unhappy." Liberation from ignorance occurs when the I-thought, through *pramāṇa*-based inquiry, with the guidance of the teacher, comes to understand its nature as limitless awareness. The essence of such valid knowledge consists of thought forms (*vṛttis*) generated by the sentences of the Upaniṣads that correspond with the nature of the self. A requisite of such knowledge is a calm and translucent mind in which the I-thought is able to understand itself as nonobjectifiable, illumining awareness, distinguishable from the body, senses, and mind, relating to all of these as subject to object, and as identical with *brahman,* the non-dual ground of all reality. The mind, like the polished mirror in Śaṅkara's analogy, becomes the locus for the thoughts that enable the I–notion to cease its identification with those things that may be objectified and know its identity with *brahman,* the subject awareness.[39] Just as one can never come to see one's face by objectifying it, but must rely upon an appropriate reflecting medium, the teachings of the Upaniṣad serve as the means of knowledge through which the I-notion comes to recognize itself as *brahman.* It is a unique method of knowing that which cannot be known through objectification.

All thoughts originate from and can be reduced or resolved back to the I-thought. The I-thought, on the other hand, can be traced back to its source in awareness, without which it ceases to be. Awareness, however, cannot be resolved or reduced into anything else. It simply is. Bondage and liberation are for the I-thought, the ego, and not for the self, which is always free. Both bondage and liberation are notional. Bondage is the notion that the self is limited and liberation is freedom from that notion.

NON-DUAL EXPERIENCE AND NON-DUAL KNOWLEDGE

It is possible that the particular thought-form (*vṛtti*) that eliminates ignorance such as "I am limitless awareness," may be resolved in the mind, resulting in a non-dual condition. This would be a state in which the distinctions of knower, object known, and process of knowing do not obtain. If such a state follows the gain of knowledge of the self from the teachings of the Upaniṣads, then ignorance would have already been destroyed, and all experiences, non-dual or otherwise, would be understood and interpreted in the light of Upaniṣadic knowledge. If a non-dual condition, however, does not follow the teachings of the Upaniṣads, such a state would not, in and of itself, eliminate ignorance about the nature of the self, since the problem of self-knowledge is not one of attaining or revealing the self, but of knowing the truth of its nature. From such a state, one returns with ignorance about the self.

It is difficult to understand how, without teaching, any experience, non-dual or otherwise, could certify the self as limitless awareness, non-dual, uncreated, identical in all beings and the constitutive ground of everything.[40] In a non-dual state, where the mind is supposedly transcended, self-knowledge, in the sense understood by Śaṅkara, does not take place.

> As in natural slumber and *samādhi,* though there is a natural eradication of differences, still owing to the persistence of the unreal nescience, differences occur over again when one wakes up, similarly it can happen here.[41]

There is no destruction of false knowledge (*mithyajñāna*) in *samādhi*, and ignorance persists after emerging from this state. Knowledge of the self does not occur in the absence of the mind, since it is only through appropriate thought forms (*vṛttis*) that ignorance is destroyed and such thoughts do not occur outside of the mind. It is not meaningful to speak of self-ignorance or self-knowledge without reference to the mind. It is important to note that the self as awareness is not opposed to the existence of ignorance about its nature. Awareness and mental ignorance about the nature of awareness are not incompatible. Ignorance is a mental condition characterized by misconceptions about the nature of the self and these are negated by knowledge in the form of *vṛttis* derived from a valid source of knowledge.

THE TEACHER AND THE TEXT

Brahman, the self, is not an object and cannot be known through the senses. Without data from the senses, inferences about *brahman* are essentially groundless. The nature of *brahman* cannot be established by observing it within one's mind, since it is awareness, illumining the mind, and cannot be objectified mentally. One cannot contemplate or meditate upon *brahman,* as a mental object, since *brahman* is the self of the meditator. The words of the Upaniṣads are held by Śaṅkara to be a valid *pramāṇa* for knowing the nature of *brahman.* These words, when imparted by a competent teacher, one who is versed in the Upaniṣads (*śrotriya*) and knows *brahman* to be his own self (*brahmaniṣṭa*), to a student whose mind is clear and tranquil and who has faith in the words of the teacher and the scripture, are capable of dispelling ignorance and bringing about direct and immediate knowledge. The elimination of ignorance about the self is liberation (*mokṣa*).

While the Upaniṣads constitute the valid source of knowledge, the role of the teacher is crucial, and the texts themselves emphasize this.[42] Both of the characteristics of the ideal teacher mentioned in the Muṇḍaka Upaniṣad (1.1.12), knowledge of the scripture and establishment in *brahman,* are important and necessary. A teacher who is well versed in the scripture, but who has not grasped the immediacy of *brahman* as her own self and who does not, therefore, see herself or others from this understanding, will, at best, impart mere words. Knowledge imparted by such a teacher will be indirect and the self may appear to be a remote entity, difficult to attain. One who is a *brahmaniṣṭha* and knows herself to be the limitless self, but is not well versed in the scriptures, may not be familiar with the methodology necessary to help the student understand the self as *brahman.*[43] She may not have the words or the skill to use words properly to impart knowledge. Knowledge of the self is immediate and fruitful when a skillful teacher who is free from ignorance instructs a qualified student. Śaṅkara almost always makes mention of the indispensability of the teacher side by side with his emphasis on the Upaniṣads as a valid source of knowledge. The traditional method of Advaita is not solitary engagement with the text, but textual inquiry with the guidance of a qualified teacher. Śaṅkara cautions that a person should not seek the knowledge of *brahman* independently "even though he is versed in the scriptures."[44]

The Vedas are understood by Śaṅkara to be revealed by *brahman.* One of his interpretations of *Brahmasūtra* 1.1.3 (*śāstrayonitvāt*), is that *brahman* is the source of the scriptures. "For scriptures like the Ṛg Veda, possessed of all good qualities, as they are," writes Śaṅkara, "cannot possibly emerge from any source other than an all-knowing One. . . . It goes without saying that the Being has absolute omniscience and omnipotence, since from Him emerge the Ṛg Veda . . . and since the emergence of these Vedas from that Being occurs as though in sport and without any effort like the breath of a man."[45] Śaṅkara approvingly cites Bṛhadāraṇyaka Upaniṣad (2.4.10), "Those that are called Ṛg Veda, (Yajur-Veda, etc.) are but the exhalation of this great Being." The Upaniṣads, which, for Śaṅkara, constitute an integral part of the Vedas, are obviously understood to have their source in *brahman.* Śaṅkara does not understand the Upaniṣadic claims about the nature of the self to be conclusions derived from human reasoning or experience since, as already noted, all such sources are inappropriate for revealing the nature of *brahman.*

From its origin in *brahman,* the knowledge of the self is preserved and transmitted through the lineage of teachers and students, referred to as the *guru-śisya paramparā.* Advaita teachers and students regularly recite a traditional verse acknowledging the origination of this knowledge in *brahman* and its flow through a succession of teachers and students.

sadāśivasamārambhāṁ śaṅkarācāryamadhyamām
asmadācāryaparyantāṁ vande guruparamparām
I salute the lineage of teachers, beginning with the ever-auspicious Śiva, Śaṅkarācārya in the middle, and extending to my own teacher.

BRAHMAN AS ULTIMATE MYSTERY

While it is our contention that the Upaniṣads are, for Śaṅkara, the definitive source of liberating knowledge, it is extremely important to emphasize that the words of the text do not reveal the intrinsic nature of *brahman.* This transcends all direct definitions and explanations. The content of liberating knowledge is the identity between the self (*ātman*) and the limitless *brahman* and *brahman* as the single ontological reality, non-different from the essential nature of everything. This is not the same as knowing the constitutive nature of *brahman. Brahman,* as Taittirīya Upaniṣad (2.9.1) reminds us, is "that from which words turn back, together with the mind." It is, in the words of Śaṅkara, "beyond all concepts and words."[46] The Upaniṣads identify *brahman* as limitless, self-existent awareness, the cause (*kāraṇa*) of the entire world (*jagat*).[47] The world, as an effect (*kārya*) of *brahman* is further characterized as essentially non-different from *brahman* and related to *brahman* as clay-effects to clay-substance.[48] Such revelations, however, are not an attempt to conventionally account for or explain the existence and constitutive nature of *brahman.* To understand that *brahman* is awareness in relation to things known does not tell us what awareness *is.* As a non-object, awareness is not available for scrutiny and analysis. Liberative knowledge must be distinguished from analytical knowledge that attempts to understand a phenomenon by identifying or breaking down its constitutent parts. Although Advaita can offer only a liberative understanding of *brahman,* Advaitins do not always admit this distinction between both types of knowledge.

The nature of *brahman* as ultimate mystery is best illustrated by Śaṅkara's unequivocal argument for the limits of commonly used terms. Although the term *sat* (being/existence/timeless), for example, is widely used in contemporary Advaita discourse to characterize *brahman,* Śaṅkara contends that *brahman* transcends the categories of being and non-being, existence and nonexistence. Such terms are only properly applicable to objects in time and space.

> That thing, indeed, which can be perceived by the senses, such as a pot, can be an object of consciousness accompanied with the idea of existence, or an object of consciousness accompanied by the idea of non-existence. Since, on the other hand, the Knowable, is beyond the reach of the senses and as such can be known solely through that instrument of knowledge which is called *Śabda,* it cannot be, like a pot, etc., an object of consciousness accompanied with the idea of either (existence or non-existence) and is therefore not said to be *sat* or *asat.*[49]

In a similar way, Śaṅkara refutes an opponent's argument that the word *consciousness* defines the essential nature of *brahman,* since it is not a feature of the elements, body, senses, or mind. Even "consciousness," claims Śaṅkara, is only a characterization of *brahman* with reference to limiting adjuncts (mind, body, senses) and does not describe the intrinsic nature of *brahman.*[50]

Perhaps the most common characterization of *brahman* in the Advaita tradition is as *ātman* (self). In his commentary on Bṛhadāraṇyaka Upaniṣad, Śaṅkara interprets the text (*ātmetyevopāsīta*) to suggest the limits of even the term *ātman,* and cites various passages affirming the ultimate indescribability of *brahman.*

> The use of the particle "iti" along with the word "Self" to which you have referred, only signifies that the truth of the Self is really beyond the scope of the term and the concept "Self." Otherwise the Śruti would only say, "One should meditate upon the Self." But this would imply that the term and concept "Self" were permissible with regard to the Self. That, however, is repugnant to the Śruti.[51]

The true natue of *brahman* eludes all definition. Its intrinsic nature can only be described by denying the validity of all descriptions as in the famous Bṛhadāraṇyaka Upaniṣad texts (2.3.6) *neti neti* (not this, not this). Paradoxically, to know *brahman* is to know it as transcending all conventional descriptions. It is this truth that the Kena Upaniṣad affirms.

> It is known to him to whom It is unknown; he does not know to whom It is known. It is unknown to those who know well, and known to those who do not know.[52]

Brahman elicits awe and wonder.

> Marvellously, someone perceives this;
> Marvellously, another declares this;
> Marvellously, still another hears of this;
> But even having heard of this, no one knows it.[53]

CHAPTER FIVE

Brahman as the World

Brahman is limitless (*ananta*) and, since the limitless cannot be two, *brahman* is regarded as non-dual. The term *advaita* actually means "non-dual" and its use is indicative of the general preference in the Upaniṣads, and in the Advaita tradition, to speak about *brahman* by describing what it is not. Since all words have finite references, the limitless *brahman* cannot be directly and positively signified by any word. Only a limited entity can be properly defined in finite language. This is the problem, for instance, with describing *brahman* as one and with characterizing Advaita as monism. Numerical categories, such as the number one, gain meaning from the existence of other numbers. When reality is non-dual, we are constrained to use such categories with caution.[1]

DENYING THE REALITY AND VALUE OF THE WORLD

If *brahman* is non-dual and limitless, how are we to understand the status and significance of the world in relation to *brahman*? Some Advaita commentators appear to suggest that the knowledge of *brahman* requires and results in the eradication of the experience of plurality.[2] The world must, in some sense, be discarded before we can discover *brahman*. "The complex world of our ordinary experience disappears in the pure white light of spiritual simplicity. All distinctions, contradictions and multiplicities are transcended and obliterated."[3]

In affirming *brahman* as absolute and limitless, the reality of the world is often denied. The world is likened to a sense-illusion, which we conjure, and experience because of our ignorance. The most famous of these analogies equates the world with a snake that is mistakenly perceived in place of a rope. "The world," as T. M. P. Mahadevan puts it, "is but an illusory appearance in *Brahman*, even as the snake is in the rope."[4] The implication here is that when the rope is properly known, the illusory snake will no longer exist. In addition, the disappearance of the snake is a condition for truly knowing the rope. Similarly, when *brahman* is known the world ceases to be, and *brahman* cannot be known as long as the world is experienced. After the reality of the world is denied, it is easy to deny meaning and value for it.

> Just as things and events seen in a dream vanish altogether and become meaningless when one wakes up, so does the universe with all its contents disappear when one finds the Real Self. One then becomes perfectly awakened to what really exists, the Absolute. Compared with That, the universe is no more than a dream. So long as one sees in a dream, the dream objects are intensely real. So also is the universe with all its contents to one under the spell of *avidyā* (ignorance). On awakening to Absolute Reality, however, all these have no value, no meaning, no existence.[5]

In his well-known work on Indian philosophy, Surendranath Dasgupta advances a similar interpretation of the view of Śaṅkara on the status of the world. "The Upaniṣads," in the words of Dasgupta, "held that reality or truth was one, and there was 'no many' anywhere, and Śaṅkara explained it by adding that the 'many' was merely an illusion, and hence did not exist in reality and was bound to disappear when the truth was known."[6]

If the world has no existence for the person who knows *brahman*, how is it possible for the liberated, the one who has attained *mokṣa*, to live in a nonexistent world? If the world has no value after liberation, what is the nature and meaning of human action for the liberated? Do human relationships have any meaning or are these ontologically equivalent, as suggested in the following story told by the Hindu teacher Ramakrishna, to experiences occurring in a dream?

> There was a farmer who lived in the countryside. He was a real *jñāni* (wise person). He was married and after many years a son was born to him, whom he named Haru. The parents loved the boy dearly. This was natural since he was the one precious gem of the family. On account of his religious nature, the farmer was loved by the villagers. One day he was working in the field when a neighbor came and told him that Haru had an attack of cholera. The farmer at once returned home and arranged for the treatment of the boy. But Haru died. The other members of the family were grief-stricken, but the farmer acted as if nothing had happened. He consoled his family and told them that grieving was futile. Then he went back to his field. On returning home, he found his wife weeping even more bitterly. She said to him: "How heartless you are! You haven't shed one tear for the child." The farmer replied quietly: "Shall I tell you why I haven't wept? I dreamt I had become a king. I was the father of eight sons and very happy with them. Then I woke up. Now I am greatly perplexed. Should I weep for these eight sons or for this one Haru?"[7]

When the reality of the world is denied, it is not consistent for one to be affected by events within it. To respond to the world is to grant reality to the world; it is to treat as real that which does not exist. Such an interpretation provides a justification for world-renunciation rather than world-affirmation, and has been most strongly and clearly articulated in the monastic strands of Hinduism.

Taken to their extremes, these positions make it difficult to take the world seriously or to speak meaningfully about the relationship between *brahman* and the world. For these reasons, there are no systematic attempts to work out the implications of such a view of reality for life in the world. Where the reality of the world is denied, its concerns do not become important. For those who cannot or do not choose to become renunciants, the Advaita tradition has not defined and clarified a mode of existence in the world which is meaningfully reconciled with its non-dual view. The life of the renunciant (*sannyāsin*) is still seen and presented as the best expression of its worldview. Yet, such definitions are necessary if the Advaita tradition is to become socially meaningful and relevant. Is it possible to formulate an understanding of the world in relation to *brahman* which can affirm the value of the world and life within it? This is one of the significant challenges for the non-dual tradition at this time and my attempt, in the present chapter, to consider this issue is a response to this challenge.

THE ORIGIN OF THE WORLD FROM *BRAHMAN*

The Advaita tradition, following the Upaniṣads, generally uses as its starting point the existence of *brahman* before all things. The uncreated, non-dual, and indivisible nature of *brahman* is underlined. The Aitareya Upaniṣad (1.1), for example, commences with an emphasis on the non-duality of *brahman* before creation.

> In the beginning this world was the self (*ātman*), one alone, and there was no other being at all that blinked an eye. He thought to himself "Let me create the worlds."[8]

In the Chandogya Upaniṣad (6.2.1–2), Āruṇi explains the teaching to his son Śvetaketu. Here, the emphasis is on the origination of the world from *brahman* and not from non-being.

> In the beginning, son, this world was simply what is existent—one only, without a second. Now on this point some do say: "In the beginning this world was simply what is non-existent—one only, without a second. And from what is non-existent was born what is existent."
>
> But, son, how can that possibly be? How can what is existent be born from what is non-existent? On the contrary, son, in the beginning this world was simply what is existent—one only, without a second.

Passages like these reveal a concern to refute the origin of the world in anything but *brahman*. Doctrines of preexistent matter and material monism are denied. In the Advaita view, there cannot be creation out of nothing, since the origin of existence from nonexistence is logically contradictory.

Some Upaniṣads even offer a description of the sequence of the emergence of the universe from *brahman*. Āruṇi, in the same dialogue from the Chāndogya Upaniṣad (6.2.3) referred to above, explains one order of creation.

> It emitted heat. The heat thought to itself: "Let me become many. Let me propagate myself." It emitted water. Whenever it is hot, therefore, a man surely perspires; and thus it is from heat that water is produced. The water thought to itself: "Let me become many. Let me propagate myself." It emitted food. Whenever it rains, therefore, food becomes abundant; and thus it is from water that food is produced.

The sequence in Taittirīya Upaniṣad (2.1.1) is even more detailed.

> From this very self (*ātman*) did space come into being; from space, air; from air, fire; from fire, the waters; from the waters, the earth; from the earth, plants, from plants, food; and from food, man.[9]

Various analogies are utilized also in the Upaniṣads to describe the emergence of the world from *brahman* and *brahman's* relationship with the world. Some of the well-known ones occur in the Muṇḍaka Upaniṣad (1.1.7 and 2.1.1):

> As a spider spins out threads, then draws them into itself;
> As plants sprout out from the earth;
> As head and body hair grows from a living man;
> So from the imperishable all things here spring.
>
> As from a well-stoked fire sparks fly by the thousands,
> all looking just like it,
> So from the imperishable issue diverse things,
> and into it, my friend, they return.

BRAHMAN AS INTELLIGENT AND MATERIAL CAUSE

While these analogies complement and enrich each other, they imply also two important aspects of the relationship between *brahman* and the world for Advaita. First, *brahman* is the intelligent or efficient cause (*nimitta kāraṇa*) for the creation of the world. Second, as all four analogies suggest, *brahman* is also the material cause (*upādāna kāraṇa*) of the universe.[10] Like a spider projecting a web from itself, but unlike a bird building its nest, *brahman* brings forth the world without the aid of anything extraneous. As already noted, the language of *creatio ex nihilo* (creation from nothing) is not employed by the Upaniṣads or the Advaita tradition to describe the emergence of the world from *brahman*. In the Advaita tradition, this doctrine becomes untenable from the perspective that nothing can be created from nothing. To preserve the unity of the absolute before creation and to deny preexistent matter, it is not necessary to argue for the creation of the world out of nothing. Such an argument appears to problematically transform "nothing" into a positive "something" which then becomes the material cause of the universe. The concern that if *brahman* is posited as both intelligent and material cause of creation, *brahman* will, in effect, be transformed into the universe and lose its original nature is, as we shall see below, addressed in Advaita.

THE UNIVERSE AS NON-DIFFERENT FROM *BRAHMAN*

Along with the suggestion that *brahman* is the sole source of the creation, there are numerous passages in the Upaniṣads affirming that the universe is non-different from *brahman*, and that all that exists is *brahman*. Kaṭha Upaniṣad (4.10–11) identifies the universe with *brahman* and denies the reality of diversity.

> Whatever is down, the same is over there;
> and what is over there is replicated down here.
> From death to death he goes, who sees
> here any kind of diversity.
> With your mind alone you must understand it—
> there is here no diversity at all!
> From death to death he goes, who sees
> here any kind of diversity.

Using the syllable *Om* to refer to *brahman*, Māṇḍūkya Upaniṣad (1–2) begins with the statement that the whole world is *Om*. The past, present, future, and anything beyond these three times is *Om*. All is *brahman*, which is identical with the self (*ātman*).[11] The Śvetāśvatara Upaniṣad (4. 2–4) poetically proclaims the identity of *brahman* and the universe.

> The fire is simply that; the sun is that; the wind is that; and the moon is also that! The bright one is simply that; *brahman* is that; the waters are that; and Prajāpati is that!
>
> You are a woman; you are a man; you are a boy or also a girl. As an old man, you totter along with a walking stick. As you are born, you turn your face in every direction.
>
> You are the dark blue bird, the green one with red eyes, the raincloud, the seasons, and the ocean. You live as one without a beginning because of your pervasiveness, you, from whom all things have been born.

The Upaniṣads emphasize also that *brahman* remains the same in spite of being the single cause of the universe. *Brahman* is not depleted, lost, or transformed by the origination of the universe. This is best illustrated in the peace verse (*śanti mantra*) found at the commencement of the Bṛhadāraṇyaka Upaniṣad.

> That is infinite,
> This is infinite.

From that infinite,
This infinite came.
From that infinite,
This infinite removed,
The infinite alone remains.[12]

In his exegesis of this famous text, Śaṅkara suggests that the universe which has come from the infinite *brahman* is not different in essential nature from *brahman*. Its origination from *brahman* does not alter or limit the nature of *brahman*. When the non-difference of the universe from *brahman* is understood, the original and infinite *brahman* still is.

What we have in the Upaniṣads then, according to Advaita, is the existence of the limitless and non-dual *brahman* before the origin of the universe, a description of the emergence of the universe from *brahman*, which is its intelligent and material cause, and thus the claim that the universe is non-different from *brahman*. *Brahman* remains limitless and non-dual after the emergence of the world. How then are we to understand and characterize the relationship between *brahman* and the world? If *brahman* is the sole cause of the world, if *brahman* has not undergone a transformation to become the world, and if the world is essentially non-different from *brahman*, then a unique explanation is called for to describe the status of the world in relation to *brahman* and its origin from *brahman*.

Non-dual *brahman* alone exists
Brahman is the sole cause for the world
Brahman does not undergo a change of nature to produce the world
World is non-different in essential nature from *brahman*.[13]

In the case of *brahman* and the world, we have a cause and effect relationship in which the cause, without any loss of nature, produces an effect from which it is essentially non-different. Since the emergence of the world does not add anything to the non-dual *brahman* or cause its transformation, the phenomenon is better characterized as that of one appearing to be many and other than what it is.[14]

THE DOCTRINE OF *MĀYĀ*

To explain this phenomenon, Advaita commentators have made extensive use of the doctrine of *māyā* to discuss the process of the one appearing as many, and more specifically, to explain the possibility of insentient (*jaḍa*) objects originating from *brahman* whose nature is awareness (*cetana*). Advaita commentators generally ascribe indirect causality to *brahman* in relation to the world. *Brahman* is presented merely as the support (*adhiṣṭhāna*) of *māyā*, which is identified as the direct material cause of the world. Unlike *brahman*, *māyā* is described as insentient (*jaḍa*), and could explain the origin of an insentient universe from *brahman*.[15] This view of the nature of *māyā* and its relationship to *brahman* has been recently described as a "post Śaṅkarite myth," which finds no justification in the commentaries of Śaṅkara.[16] This popular Advaita understanding which traces the origin of the world to *māyā*, and only indirectly to *brahman* as the support of *māyā*, has contributed, I believe, to the devaluation of the world and to the reduction of its significance. The questioning of this interpretation is therefore, significant.[17]

Śaṅkara traces the origin of the world to *brahman* alone.

> That omniscient and omnipotent source must be *brahman* from which occur the birth, continuance, and dissolution of this universe that is manifested through name and form, that is associated with diverse agents and experiences, that provides the support for actions and results, having well-regulated space, time and causation, and that defies all thoughts about the real nature of its creation.[18]

He repeatedly refutes the Sāṅkhyan cosmology that proposes that insentient matter (*prakṛti*) is the material cause of the universe. "The universe," writes Śaṅkara, "cannot possibly be thought of as having its origin etc., from any other factor, e.g. *pradhāna* (primordial nature) which is insentient, or from atoms, or non-existence, or some soul under worldy conditions (viz., *hiraṇyagarbha*). Nor can it originate spontaneously; for in this universe people (desirous of products) have to depend on specific space, time and causation."[19] It is clear that any attempt to explain the world by positing its origin in a material cause other than *brahman* is contrary to Śaṅkara's viewpoint. *Brahman*, for Śaṅkara, is the sole efficient and material cause for creation.

Śaṅkara's argument in *Brahmasūtra* (2.1.24) is relevant here also. He is responding to the claim that *brahman* cannot be the cause of the world since *brahman* possesses no accessories (viz., materials) and accessories are necessary for creation. While admitting that accessories are needed by limited beings, Śaṅkara contends that *brahman* "is possessed of the fullest power, and It has not to depend on anything else for imparting an excellence (to that power). . . . Hence even though *brahman* is one, it is possible for It, by virtue of the possession of diverse powers, to be transformed variously. . . ."[20] This argument also rules out *māyā* as a material accessory or as an accessory of any kind necessary for the creation of the world.

If *brahman* and not *māyā* is understood by Śaṅkara to be the cause of the world, how is it possible for *brahman*, whose nature is awareness, to bring forth a world which is insentient? This question becomes particularly important in the light of Śaṅkara's view that the effect is non-different from the cause.[21] The well-known answer to this question is the proposition of the insentient *māyā* as the material cause of the universe, an answer that finds no justification in Śaṅkara in the light of his refutation of any cause other than the non-dual *brahman*.[22] To resolve the dilemma of effects being essentially non-different from their causes and the sentient *brahman* being the cause of the insentient world, Srinivasa Rao questions the meaning of insentiency (*acetana / jada*) in Śaṅkara and differentiates it from the Sāṅkhyan view.[23] For Sāṅkhya, which is radically dualistic, *puruṣa* is sentient (*cetana*) and *prakṛti*, which is the material cause of the world, is insentient (*jada*). Their natures are opposed to each other. For Advaita, on the other hand, which affirms the truth of the non-dual *brahman* alone, reality does not consist of different ontological entities with contrasting natures. For Advaita, the insentient (*acetana*) "cannot be construed as something that *fundamentally lacks* sentiency; it can only be construed as something that does not manifestly reveal its sentiency. It must be noted that what does not manifestly reveal sentiency is not necessarily the same as what is fundamentally insentient in nature."[24] If the world is not different in its essential nature from *brahman*, there is no need to propose a cause other than *brahman*. The world may be regarded as the expression or manifestation of *brahman*. This means that the world does not have an existence that is independent of *brahman*, its sole cause.

ASYMMETRICAL RELATIONSHIP BETWEEN *BRAHMAN* AND WORLD

While denying the independent existence of the world from *brahman* and affirming its origin and essential non-difference (*ananyatva*) from *brahman*, Śaṅkara does not go to the other extreme and fully equate the world with *brahman*. The fact that *brahman* is described as the cause and the world as the effect implies some difference. If there were no differences, the distinction would be meaningless.

> As between cause and effect, some distinction has got to be admitted as existing, as in the case of clay and a pot, for unless some peculiarity exists, it is not possible to distinguish them as cause and effect.[25]

The nonmanifestation of awareness in objects of the world does not refute the origin of everything in *brahman*. In support of his argument that *brahman* alone is the intelligent and material cause of the world, Śaṅkara offers an illustration to establish the possibility of effects that appear to be different from their causes. "The assertion that this universe does not have *brahman* as its material cause, since its characteristics are different," writes Śaṅkara, "is not wholly true. For it is a matter of common experience that from a man, well-known as a conscious being, originate hair, nail etc., that are different in nature (being insentient), and scorpions etc., grow in cow-dung etc., known to be insentient."[26] While the analogy is odd, the point is clear. *Brahman* can be the cause of a world that possesses characteristics different from *brahman*.

The relationship between *brahman* as cause and the world as effect is an asymmetrical one.[27] The world, as an effect of *brahman*, shares in the nature of *brahman*. Existence, for example, which is fundamental to *brahman*, is shared by all objects in the world.[28] The characteristics of the world, however, do not constitute the essential nature of *brahman*. "The effect," as Śaṅkara, puts it, "has the nature of the cause and not vice-versa."[29] While the world partakes of the nature of *brahman*, *brahman* does not partake of the nature of the world.[30]

We may illustrate this point with the help of two analogies used in the Upaniṣads.[31] The teacher, Āruṇi, employs the example of clay and various objects made from it to help his son, Śvetaketu, understand *brahman* as the material basis of the world. Clay is the material cause of various objects such as jars, etc., that share the basic nature of clay. Clay, in the form of a jar, still retains its essential nature as clay and, in this sense, the jar may be said to be non-different from clay. The jar, however, possesses some characteristics that do not belong to the essential nature of clay. The unique shape of the jar, for example, does not belong to the clay as clay. If the roundness of the jar is considered an essential characteristic of clay, all clay would be round. The same is true for gold and various ornaments fashioned out of gold. Although the ornaments are made of gold, the specific shape of each ornament does not define the nature of gold. It is possible, therefore, for an effect to possess characteristics that do not belong intrinsically to its cause. While the world, as an effect, is non-different in its essential nature from *brahman*, its cause, it has features that cannot be said to belong inherently to *brahman*. The world is non-different (*ananya*) from *brahman*, but *brahman* is not identical with the world.

Śaṅkara illustrates the argument that effects possess characteristics that do not belong to their causes in another way. When the unique qualities of the effects are destroyed, they do not become part of the nature of their causes. These belong only to the effects.

> For instance, such products as plates etc., fashioned out of the material earth have peculiarities of being high, medium and flat during their separate existence; but when they become re-absorbed into their original substance, they do not transfer their individual features to it. Nor do products as necklaces etc., fashioned out of gold transfer their individual peculiarities to gold during their merger into it.[32]

By admitting, as Śaṅkara clearly does, that the world possesses characteristics that do not belong to the nature of *brahman*, do we not compromise the non-duality of *brahman*? Do we not admit the existence of something other than *brahman*? To help answer this question, let us return to our analogies of clay and gold and their various products. In clarifying how the knowledge of a clod of clay leads to the knowledge of all products made from clay, Śaṅkara explains that the effect is non-different from its cause. The difference between one clay product and another is a difference of name and form (*nāmarūpa vikāra*) and differences of name and form, in this viewpoint, do not constitute a difference in the essential nature of the object. "The features of an effect are never strong enough to confer a separate ontological identity on that effect—an identity that would allow us to legitimately describe that effect as something really different from its cause. The effect is always ontologically parasitic on its cause for its own identity. But, the cause, despite producing an effect, retains its own ontological identity and independence."[33] The truth of non-duality is thus preserved, even though one admits the effect to have characteristics different from the cause.

If a modification of name and form is not enough to confer separate ontological identity on an effect, a change of name and form is not a change in the intrinsic nature of the cause. When gold ornaments are made from gold, the change involved is understood to be in name and form (*nāmarūpa*) alone. There is no change in the original or essential nature of gold. Similarly, when the world emerges from *brahman*, which is its intelligent and material cause, the nature of *brahman* is not lost or transformed. Without undergoing any loss or depletion of nature, *brahman* brings forth the world from itself.[34]

IS THE WORLD AN ILLUSION?

Śaṅkara does not describe the world as an illusion, and it is not often remembered that he argued strongly against the subjective idealists who reduce the world to a mere idea of the perceiving individual and who deny the world any existence outside of the mind. He challenges the claim that what appears to be outside the mind is an illusion and argues for the objective nature of the world.

> For external things are perceived as a matter of fact. It is wrong to say that external things do not exist merely on the ground that cognition is seen to have the likeness of an object, because the very likeness of an object is not possible unless the object itself be there, and also because the object is cognized outside.[35]

Perhaps even more important is the fact that he objects to any equation between waking and dream experiences. The significant difference is that dream experiences and perceptions are contradicted in the waking state, whereas the experiences of the latter are not negated in any state. One is sublatable while the other is not. This distinction that Śaṅkara makes between the dream-reality and waking-reality is most significant in view of the common equation between the two made by Advaita interpreters. His comment on the difference between both is worth citing at length.

> To a man arisen from sleep, the object perceived in a dream becomes sublated, for he says, "Falsely did I imagine myself in contact with great men. In fact I never came in contact with great men; only my mind became overpowered by sleep; and thus this delusion arose." So also in the case of magic etc., adequate sublation takes place. But a thing seen in the waking state, a pillar for instance, is not thus sublated under any condition. Moreover dream vision is a kind of memory, whereas the visions of the waking state are forms of perception (through valid means of knowledge). And the difference between perception and memory, consisting in the presence and absence of objects can be understood by oneself, as for instance when one says, "I remember

> my beloved son, but I do not see him, though I want to see." That being so, it cannot be asserted by a man, who feels the difference of the two, that the perception of the waking state is false, merely on the ground that it is a perception like the perception in a dream. And it is not logical for those who consider themselves intelligent to deny their own experience. Moreover, one who cannot speak of the waking experiences as naturally baseless, just because this would contradict experience, wants to speak of them as such on the strength of their similarity with dream experiences. But anything that cannot be the characteristic of something in its own right, cannot certainly be so because of a similarity with another. For fire which is felt to be warm does not become cold because of some similarity with water.[36]

What Śaṅkara emphatically denies is that the world has a reality and existence independent of *brahman*. The world derives its reality from *brahman*, whereas the reality of *brahman* is independent and original. The world does not have an existence of its own, whereas *brahman's* existence is its own.[37] Illuminating in this context is Śaṅkara's differentiation of various ontological levels.[38] The significance of these becomes clearer in the light of the Advaita notion of sublation (*bādha*). Sublation is "the activity of rectifying errors of judgment concerning fact or value."[39] It is the "mental process whereby one disvalues some previously appraised object or content of consciousness because of its being contradicted by a new experience."[40] If one rushes toward a shining object on the road, thinking that it is a precious jewel, but then discovers that it is a piece of broken glass, one's earlier judgment is sublated by one's discovery.

Four ontological levels are distinguished in Advaita. *Unreality* is that which does not exist in any period of time, past, present, or future. An unreal object, such as a square circle, is neither sublatable nor non-sublatable. The world clearly does not belong to this category. *Illusory reality* (*prātibhāsika sattā*) is sublatable. Optical and sensory illusions, such as mistaking a rope for a snake, or a piece of broken glass for jewelry, as well as dream experiences, belong to this category. We have already noted that Śaṅkara differentiates the world from this order of reality, since illusions and dreams are subjective and sublatable whereas the individual never sublates the world.[41] Water is real in comparison to mirage-water, which is false.[42] Since illusory objects do not have objective existence, they cease to exist when they are contradicted. The snake that is perceived in place of the rope vanishes when the rope is discerned.

Empirical or pragmatic reality (*vyavahārika satta*) is the category to which the world belongs, while *absolute reality* (*pāramārthika sattā*) is the ontological status of *brahman*. When the truth of *brahman's* non-duality is understood, the world, unlike an illusion, does not cease to be. A false view of the universe, and not the universe itself, is destroyed. One who understands *brahman* no longer commits the error of assuming the world to have a reality and existence independent of *brahman*. One understands the world to be of the nature of *brahman* while not superimposing (*adhyāsa*) the nature of the world on *brahman*. The world is understood to be non-different in essential nature from *brahman*. Unlike a dream in relation to waking, however, the world does not cease to be as a consequence of the knowledge of *brahman*. "Just as *brahman*, the cause is never without existence in all three periods of time, so also the universe, which is the effect, never parts with existence in all three periods. But Existence is only one."[43]

In his commentary on *Brahmasūtra* 3.2.21, Śaṅkara summarizes an opponent's argument that the knowledge of *brahman* cannot occur without the sublation of the world. Even as darkness obscures the perception of an object and has to be removed by one who wishes to see the object, contends the opponent, the world stands opposed to *brahman* and has to be sublated by one who is desirous of knowing *brahman*.[44] Śaṅkara, in his response, clarifies what the sublation of the world means.

> What is meant by this sublation of the universe of manifestations? Is the world to be annihilated like the destruction of the solidity of *ghee* by contact with fire; or is it that the world of name and form, created in *brahman* by nescience like many moons created in the moon by the eye-disease called *timira*, has to be destroyed through knowledge? Now if it be said that this existing universe of manifestations, consisting of the body etc., on the corporeal plane and externally of the earth etc., is to be annihilated, that is a task impossible for any man, and hence the instruction about its extirpation is meaningless. Moreover, (even supposing that such a thing is possible, then) the universe, including the earth etc., having been annihilated by the first man who got liberation, the present universe should have been devoid of the earth etc.[45]

The world, according to Śaṅkara, exists both for the one who knows *brahman* and the one who does not know *brahman*. The difference is that the knower of *brahman* understands the world, despite its appearance, to be non-different, in essential nature, from *brahman* and to be dependent on *brahman* for its existence and reality.[46] D. M. Datta correctly summarizes Śaṅkara's position when he writes that, with the knowledge of *brahman*, "the differentiated world of ordinary experience stands transfigured, as the manifestation of Brahman, when attention is diverted from multiplicity to the unity of the whole universe and the ordinary judgement is revised in the light of the new experience of intuition of the one. So, the negation of the world, as conceived by Śaṅkara, is more a transformation, re-organization and revaluation than wholesale annihilation."[47]

WORLD AS CELEBRATIVE EXPRESSION OF *BRAHMAN*

The Advaita tradition, as systematized by Śaṅkara, does not fully equate the world, as an effect, with *brahman*, its intelligent and material ground. It does not also grant the world a nature and reality that is independent of *brahman*. We have discussed the Advaita argument that "though the cause and effect are non-different, the effect has the nature of the cause and not vice-versa."[48] While the world is non-different from *brahman*, *brahman* is different from the world. Avoiding both extremes, Advaita admits that the world in its relationship to *brahman* is an indefinable mystery (*anirvacanīya*). Although analogies of various kinds are used, both in the Upaniṣads and by Śaṅkara, to illustrate the emergence of the world from and its relationship with *brahman*, no analogy is entirely adequate to the task. Upaniṣadic analogies are illustrative and not definitive, suggestive and not descriptive. Clay and gold are finite objects within space and time and their transformation into pots and jewelery cannot fully explain how the world comes from *brahman*. *Brahman* is limitless and non-dual and has no analogical parallel. Analogies are aids to understanding, but these are not meant to fully explain the relationship between *brahman* and the world.

Without any diminution and loss of nature (*svarūpa*), *brahman* brings the world out of itself. The origin of the world from *brahman* is likened to the emergence of name and form, which does not give to the world an independent ontological status. It is not *brahman* plus something else, but *brahman* inexplicably appearing as the world. If a change of name and form does not bring into existence a new reality, it does not also bring about a transformation in the essential nature of the cause or deplete it in any way.

To argue that the world, as an effect, enjoys a dependent relation to its cause, *brahman*, is not to deny it meaning and value. On the contrary, since *brahman* has ultimate value, the relationship of non-difference between the world and *brahman* enriches the value of the world. It is unfortunate that some interpreters of the Advaita tradition have used the world's dependent status to enthusiastically explain it away. Too much energy has been expended in traditional Adviata metaphysics in establishing the so-called unreality of the world. The world, in itself, is neither illusory nor deceptive. The world simply is. Ignorance is a human characteristic because of which one fails to apprehend the non-difference of the world from *brahman*. Ignorance is overcome when we understand the world to be the indefinable expression of *brahman*. The world is a celebrative expression of *brahman's* fullness, an overflow of *brahman's* undiminishing limitlessness. It value is derived from the fact that it partakes of the nature of *brahman* even though, as a finite process, it can never fully express *brahman*. In fact, the world, as non-different from *brahman*, enjoys the same permanency and reality as *brahman*. In the words of Śaṅkara, "Just as the *brahman*, the cause, is never without existence in all three periods of time, so also the universe, which is an effect, never parts company with Existence in all the three periods."[49]

It is not at all necessary to deny the reality and value of the world in order to affirm the non-duality and limitlessness of *brahman*. The need to do this arises from the wrong assertion, in the first instance, of the separateness of the world from *brahman*. We do not need to deny the many in order to affirm the one, when ontological non-duality is affirmed and when the many is seen as non-different from the one. The precise Advaita teaching is that the world emerges from *brahman*, is sustained by *brahman*, and returns to *brahman* without, in any way, limiting or diminishing *brahman*. In the example of gold and gold ornaments, the ornament does not have to be denied in order to recover gold, since the ornament is non-different from gold and gold has not lost its nature with the coming into being of the ornament. If gold lost its nature in the creation of the ornament, the denial of the latter would not restore the gold.

The problem is not the world itself, but attributing to the world an existence that is independent of *brahman*. There is too much negative emphasis in the Advaita tradition on the falsity and deceptive character of the world and too little positive celebration of the world as an expression of *brahman*. This problem has arisen, in part, because of post-Śaṅkara interpretations that attribute only indirect causality to *brahman* as the substratum (*adhiṣṭhāna*) of *māyā*. *Māyā*, with its historical overtones of illusion, deceptivity, untruth, and falsehood, is posited as the true material cause of the world, and the world, as the product of *māyā*, is problematized and devalued. *Māyā* is used to disconnect the world from *brahman* in order to secure *brahman* as limitless and non-dual. Śaṅkara, however, never describes the world as the creation of *māyā* (*māyaprakṛtika*) but consistently as the creation of *brahman* (*brahmaprakṛtika*). This is his main argument against the Sāṅkhya tradition that traces the origin of the world to insentient matter (*jaḍaprakṛti*).

To understand the world as an effect of and as non-different from *brahman* does not require us to grant the same value to the world as we do to *brahman*. It does not require us to also dismiss the world as without value. Ultimate value belongs to *brahman*, the origin and source of the created order. The world gains its value from the fact that it is an expression of *brahman* and ultimately non-different in nature from *brahman*. As a finite expression, it does not fully express *brahman* and cannot, therefore, enjoy the same value as *brahman*. *Brahman* is always greater than the sum total of its created effects and enjoys ultimate value.

SEEING THE ONE *AND* THE MANY

Avidyā (ignorance) is to see the many and to be blind to the One. *Avidyā*, however, is also to think that the seeing of the One requires the devaluing and negation of the many. It is particularly instructive to note that authoritative texts describing the liberated understanding consistently present it as a way of seeing both *brahman* and the world. There is no suggestion that the world is nonexistent in the vision of the liberated. Typical of such texts are the following from the Bhagavadgītā (6:30; 13:28; 18:20).[50]

> One who sees me everywhere and sees everything in me is not lost to me, nor will I be lost to him.

> One who sees the great Lord existing equally in all beings, the imperishable in the persishable, truly sees.
>
> That knowledge by which one sees one imperishable being in all beings, indivisible in the divisible, is the highest (*sattvic*).

Texts such as these invite a way of seeing reality that does not require negation of the world of plurality, but a celebration of its relationship with *brahman*. Meaning and value are added, not taken, from the world, when its ontological unity and inseparable existence from *brahman* is affirmed.

CHAPTER SIX

Brahman as God

In the previous chapter, we considered the status of the world in relation to *brahman.* While the world cannot express fully the nature of *brahman,* it partakes in the nature of *brahman* and derives its value from this fact. The world is not an illusory projection of the human mind and Śaṅkara does not equate it with the reality of a dream. Unlike mental illusions, which cease to exist when they are contradicted, the world does not disappear when *brahman* is known. What disappears is the erroneous understanding that the world has a reality and existence that is independent of *brahman.* The fundamental characteristic of right knowledge is understanding the world to be non-different in its essential nature from *brahman.* Since *brahman's* non-duality is not compromised by the existence of the world, it does not have to be recovered by the negation of the world.

We also considered the problems of positing *māyā* to be the material cause of the universe. If the world is regarded as truly insentient, then the need arises to propose a cause other than *brahman,* since *brahman* is, by nature, sentient. For the Advaita tradition, however, the world does not enjoy an existence and a reality that is independent of *brahman.* Reality is not comprised of the sentient *brahman* plus the world, which is fundamentally insentient. Reality is ultimately *brahman* alone. The world, as a limited entity, does not fully express *brahman,* nor does it possess an essential nature that is different from or independent of *brahman. Brahman* is capable, without the aid of any other cause, of expressing itself in multiple forms and names. These names and forms, as discussed above, have characteristics that do not constitute the nature of *brahman,* but they do not possess an ontological status independent of *brahman.* As a term for the inexplicable process of how the One, without any transformation or loss of nature (*svarūpa*), assumes various forms, *māyā* has a place in the metaphysics of Advaita. Its significance, however, would only be epistemic and not ontological.[1] This distinction is not consistently clarified in Advaita and many Advaita commentators, while claiming that *māyā* is epistemic, go on to great lengths in treating it as having ontological reality. *Māyā* may also be an appropriate term to describe the fact that reality is not what it appears to be. While each object in the world appears to have an independent nature and reality, the truth is that nothing exists apart from *brahman.*

BRAHMAN AS *NIRGUṆA* AND *SAGUṆA*

When *māyā* is granted independent ontological status in Advaita, commentators distinguish between two orders or levels of *brahman* and suggest a hierarchy between these two. One is *parā* or higher *brahman* and the other is *aparā* or lower *brahman.*[2] The higher *brahman* is presented as *nirguṇa brahman,* the absolute, non-dual *brahman,* transcending time, space, causation, and relations. It is beyond all change and action and free from all names and forms. *Nirguṇa brahman,* as defined above, cannot be the source of the world, since it is considered to be beyond causation and activity.[3] One Advaita writer cogently summarized this claim.

> On the one hand there is *brahman* which is One only, which is formless, attributeless, and actionless. On the other, there is the world of perceivable objects, diverse in name and form. That is the phenomenal world, the world of the many. *Brahman* is One; the world is many. *Brahman* is attributeless, *nirguṇa;* objects are qualified by attributes, they are *saguṇa. Brahman* has no name or form; objects have different forms and names. *Brahman* is inactive and permanent; the objects of the world are active and subject to change. What is the link between the two? What is the *modus operandi* of the transition of the One into the many?[4]

The *modus operandi* or connecting principle between *brahman* and the world, according to this writer, is *māyā.* Without *māyā, nirguṇa brahman* cannot make the transition from impersonal awareness to personal creator. It is *brahman* associated with *māyā* that is the origin and source of the world. *Brahman* associated with *māyā* is referred to as *saguṇa brahman* and belongs to the lower (*aparā*) order or level. *Brahman* associated with *māyā* is also referred to as *īśvara,* the lord of creation. In this point of view, the word, *God* is used more appropriately for *īśvara* and not for *nirguṇa brahman. Īśvara* or *saguṇa brahman* is regarded by Advaita interpreters as lower *(aparā)* because, among other things, it is conditioned and related to the world. "*Saguṇa brahman* is God as appearance and not as reality."[5] *Īśvara* is related to the world and defined through that relationship, whereas *nirguṇa brahman* is *brahman*-in-itself and beyond all definitions. It is higher because it is neither cause nor effect.

> *Brahman*-in-itself is neither the cause nor the effect of anything. If it is the effect of something else, then it has a beginning, and whatever has a beginning must have an end. It means that it will cease to be eternal. If it is the cause of anything, then it becomes relational. In that case, it is no better than the things of the world which are relational.[6]

The association of *brahman* with *māyā* represents a climb down in the status of *brahman.* Whereas there is no distinction between substance and attributes in *nirguṇa brahman, saguṇa brahman* possesses attributes (*guṇas*), and this is another reason for characterizing *saguṇa brahman* as lower.[7] Advaita interpreters also tend to equate *saguṇa brahman* with the God of theistic traditions and present such traditions as advocates of a lower truth.

> *Brahman* so conceived of is God (*Ishvara*), as understood in all theistic traditions, Western and non-Western alike. It is obvious that such a conception belongs to the lower, conventional, relative, conditioned, practical standpoint; whereas the the inconceivable *Brahman* devoid of form, name, qualities, and relations, belongs to the higher, absolute standpoint. *Saguna Brahman* is God (*Ishvara*) understood as the cause, creator, sustainer, destroyer and judge of the world. It is *Saguna Brahman* that people worship in different forms and names, such as Rama, Krishna, Siva, Jesus, Allah, Jehovah, and so on. It is God as *Saguna Brahman* that is endowed with such qualities as love, kindness, and mercy. . . . But since form, name, qualities, and relations can only belong in the realm of appearances (phenomena), *Saguna Brahman* (God) is only an appearance, although the highest among appearances, and not reality.[8]

ARE HIERARCHIES IN *BRAHMAN* NECESSARY?

The description of *brahman* as *nirguṇa* and *saguṇa* is not without problems and, in spite of its dominance in Advaita rhetoric, deserves reconsideration. It presents a bifurcation in the nature of *brahman* that is inconsistent with its non-dual nature. Such a distinction is particularly problematic when there is a hierarchical ordering and one is considered to be higher (*parā*) and the other lower (*aparā*). Surely *brahman's* nature does not admit of distinctions of any kind, and the necessity and purpose of such a distinction must be queried. Does such a distinction imply that it is a part of *īśvara's* self-consciousness to regard *brahman* as having two levels of being, one higher and the other lower, and to identify with the lower?

In the previous chapter, we questioned the positing of *māyā* as the material cause of creation. Since the world does not have a nature that is other than *brahman,* there is no need to propose its origin in anything but *brahman.* Without any loss of nature, *brahman* brings forth the world of names and forms. We may use *māyā* epistemically to describe this unique process but not ontologically as the material cause of the world. It seems to me that the main purpose of Advaita interpreters, in proposing a higher and lower *brahman,* is to account for the origin of the universe in an intelligent being, *brahman*, while, at the same time, insulating or protecting *brahman* from what these interpreters perceive to be the drawbacks of ascribing creatorship to *brahman.* Creatorship, and all that it implies, thus belongs to *saguṇa brahman* while *nirguṇa brahman* is entirely free from all involvement in the world process, except as the ground or substratum (*adhiṣṭhāna*) of the creative process. But is the insulation of *brahman* from what are perceived to be the "defects" of creatorship necessary through the proposition of a higher and lower nature? This question will be answered better by considering the so-called "defects" of creatorship from which *brahman* must be kept free.

THE PROBLEM OF CHANGE AND ACTIVITY IN *BRAHMAN*

Let us begin by considering the issue of change and activity. Since the act of creation appears to imply change and activity and *brahman,* by definition, is free from all change and activity, *brahman* cannot be directly involved in the world process. Such involvement is for the lower or *saguṇa brahman.* What is interesting here is that the Advaita tradition, which is particuarly concerned, in the concept of *nirguṇa brahman,* with deconstructing anthropomorphic understandings of *brahman,* raises a problem that is generated precisely by the anthropomorphic imagination. When human beings, limited by time and space, engage in action, such action necessarily implies change. The same, however, ought not to be assumed for *brahman,* who brings forth the world without any loss or change in nature. Greater difficulties are often generated by solutions proposed for unnecessary problems. There is no need, in other words, to suggest a hierarchical bifurcation in the nature of *brahman* in order to preserve *brahman's* limitlessness.

The many analogies used in the Upaniṣads to discuss the relationship between *brahman* and the world, such as clay and pots, or gold and ornaments, make this same point. The world does not emerge from *brahman* in the same manner that gold ornaments are manufactured from gold. Gold is, after all, a limited object, in time and space. The point of the analogy is that the fundamental nature of gold remains the same in spite of the production of multiple ornaments that are non-different from gold. Since gold is always gold, even with various ornaments, there is no need to propose a distinction in the nature of gold for the purpose of preserving its original nature. In a similar way, since the creation of the world from *brahman* does not deplete or transform its nature, an explanation that involves the suggestion of a dual nature is unnecessary. Being the cause of the created world does not diminish *brahman*'s fullness of being. The value and significance of the world is surely reduced if it is felt that any kind of involvement of *brahman* in the world process implies a "climb down" on *brahman's* part. It seems contradictory to want to argue that the world partakes of the the nature of *brahman* while, at the same time, attempting, through the notion of a higher and lower *brahamn,* to disassociate *brahman* from the world.

The Upaniṣads are not at all reticent about the use of terminology suggesting action on the part of *brahman. Brahman* is described as desiring, deliberating, creating, and entering into all that is created.[9] These texts do not see the need to suggest hierarchies; the activity of *brahman* is represented as non-pareil. It is activity without ontological change or loss of nature. Īśa Upaniṣad (4–5) describes the activity of *brahman* in a series of paradoxes:

> Although not moving, the one is swifter than the mind;
> the gods cannot catch it, as it speeds on in front.
> Standing, it outpaces others who run;
> within it Mātariśvan places the waters.
>
> It moves—yet it does not move
> It is far away—yet it is near at hand!
> It is within this whole world—yet
> It is also outside this whole world.

"Sitting down," says Kaṭha Upaniṣad (2:21), "he roams afar. Lying down, he goes everywhere." In a well-known sequence of verses in the Bhagavadgītā (13:15–17), Kṛṣṇa enunciates the mystery of *brahman*, which is immanent and yet transcendent, involved in the world process and free from its finitude and limits.

> Shining by the functions of the senses, yet freed from all the senses, unattached yet maintaining all, free from the qualities yet experiencing the qualities;
>
> Outside and inside beings, those that are moving and not moving, because of its subtlety, This is not comprehended. This is far away and also near.
>
> Undivided yet remaining as if divided in all beings, This is to be known as the sustainer of beings, their devourer and creator.

There is a clear concern in the Upaniṣads to establish that *brahman* can be related to the world while at the same time not be limited by such relations. Kaṭha Upaniṣad (5:11), for instance, uses the example of the sun, which, though helping the eyes to see, is not tainted by the defects of the eyes or any other object, to illustrate how *brahman* is in all things and yet free from their limits. It is difficult to agree with the argument, cited above by R. Balasubramanian, that if *brahman* is the cause of anything it becomes relational and, because of such relations, it is no better than things of the world. *Brahman,* as we are contending, can be the intelligent and material ground of creation without suffering a loss of nature, and its relation with the world does not imply limits of the kind alluded to by Balasubramanian. Its relationship with the world, as the Upaniṣads suggest, does not reduce it to a worldly object. Advaita commentators, unfortunately, seem to think that having a relation with the world is problematic without considering the uniqueness of the *brahman*-world relationship articulated in the Upaniṣads.[10]

The characteristics belonging to the action of a finite being in time and space, cannot be attributed to *brahman,* the one in whom time and space exist. Here also we must be deeply cognizant of the limits of all words when applied to *brahman.* The finitude of language must be negated when used for *brahman,* and this includes words suggesting action. We cannot affirm that it moves, without stating that it moves not. We cannot characterize it as unmoving without adding that it is swifter than the mind.[11] If we admit this, we can speak of *brahman* as active without the need to create dual hierarchies and attribute such action to a lower *brahman,* thus devaluing action and the world. It seems to me possible, and preferable, to speak of *brahman* as active while, at the same time, denying that such activites imply limitations. The need to suggest a lower *brahman,* with all the difficulties involved, is then obviated.

THE PROBLEM OF SUBSTANCE AND ATTRIBUTES

Another reason advanced for granting a lower status to *saguṇa brahman* is the argument that whereas there is no distinction between substance and attributes (*guṇas*) in *nirguṇa brahman, saguṇa brahman* possesses attributes, and there exists a distinction of substance and attributes. The nature of this argument requires careful scrutiny since it further underlines the questionable dichotomy in the nature of *brahman* to which we alluded earlier.

Brahman is consistently described in the Upaniṣads as one only and non-dual.[12] This is interpreted by the tradition to mean that *brahman* is free from limitations of all kinds. Since *brahman* is all-pervasive, it is free from the spatial limitation (*deśa pariccheda*) which characterizes created objects. *Brahman* is not an object *in* space. As an entity that has existed and will always exist without any loss of nature, *brahman* is not subject to time limitation (*kāla pariccheda*). Since it constitutes the essential nature of everything that exists, *brahman* is free from the limitation of being one object (*vastu pariccheda*) separate and distinguishable from every other object. It is infinite *(ananta)* in all senses of the term.

The non-dual nature of *brahman* is also interpreted to mean that *brahman* is free from distinctions (*bheda*) of all kinds. In the Advaita tradition, three such distinctions are particularly highlighted. First, there is the distinction obtaining among objects belonging to different species such as plants and animals (*vijātīya bheda*). *Brahman* is free from distinctions of this kind since there is no object that enjoys a separate ontological existence and nature from *brahman.* As Chāndogya Upaniṣad (3.14.1) states it, "all is *brahman.*" Second, there is the distinction existing among different objects belonging to the same species (*svajātiya bheda*). *Brahman,* however, is not the name for a species and there are no objects similar but different from *brahman.* Distinctions of this kind, therefore, do not apply. Third, there is the distinction obtaining within a single object comprised of different parts and qualities (*svagata bheda*). A cow, for example, has legs, a tail, ears, and a head. It also has a color, shape, and size. It is internally differentiated. *Brahman,* on the other hand, has no internal distinctions. It is not a compound of diverse parts, and beyond all distinctions such as substance and attributes or whole and parts. *Brahman* is simple, indivisible, and partless.[13] Its nature transcends all definitions that are based on distinctions.

It is in the context of denying differences and distinctions of all kinds in the nature of *brahman* that the use of the term *nirguṇa* (lit., without qualities) must be understood. It emphasizes that *brahman* cannot be thought of in the manner of limited objects, and that *brahman's* nature is unique. *Nirguṇa* particularly denies the distinction of substance and attribute in *brahman.* This does not mean that one should regard *brahman* as a substance with no attributes. It means that *brahman* transcends the categories of both substance and attribute, as well as the distinction obtaining between them. Most importantly, there is nothing inherent in the idea of *nirguṇa* that rules out the possibility of *brahman's* creatorship and the world originating from *brahman.*

The term *nirguṇa* reminds us about the limits of conventional language in describing *brahman.* Words, according to Śaṅkara, define objects in four ways. They do so through categories denoting genus, actions, quality, and relation. Words such as *cow* and *horse* imply genus, *cook* and *teacher* suggest action, *red* and *blue* indicate qualites, and *wealth* and *cattleowner* point to a relation or possession.[14] *Brahman* does not belong to a species and, as already indicated, is beyond the distinction of substance and attribute. While it is the source of the world, it does not undergo a change of nature or become related to the world in ways that are limiting. Since activity and relation usually imply change, conventional words have to be used cautiously in speaking about *brahman.* The term *nirguṇa* should not to be used to disconnect *brahman* from the world and to present it as a bland and static reality incapable, unless conjoined with *māyā,* of bringing forth the creation. The essential point is that, just as *brahman* can bring forth the world from itself without suffering a loss of nature or being limited by the world, the creative act does not also affect the essential unity of *brahman's* nature, which remains always free from distinctions of every kind. We can indeed speak of *brahman* as cause and the world as effect without implying that this reduces *brahman* to a worldly entity.

The Advaita tradition, following the Upaniṣads, distinguishes clearly between the mental concepts and images we have about *brahman* and the reality of *brahman's* nature. The Taittirīya Upaniṣad twice (2.4.1 and 2.9.1) describes *brahman* as that from which all words, with the mind, return, having failed to reach.[15] Even the Vedas, in speaking about *brahman,* are constrained to use conventional words derived from everyday usage and, since these emerge from our experiences of finitude, they can never directly signify *brahman.* While conventional words are unavoidable, conventional meanings have to be avoided. Words are mere pointers to that which is beyond the meaning of all words and definitions. The need to diffferentiate between a lower and a higher *brahman* betrays this significant Advaita insight about the limits of language in relation to *brahman.*

Nirguṇabrahman, it is argued, transcends the distinction between substance and quality and is higher, whereas *saguṇabrahman* possesses attributes and is lower. The point, however, is that if the unity of *brahman's* nature precludes distinctions of all kinds, including, as already seen, the distinction of substance and quality, the act of creating the world does not cause distinctions in *brahman.* The essential nature of *brahman* is the same before and after the world comes into existence. In relation to creation, we must rightly speak of *brahman* as creator, lord, support, and as omniscient and omnipotent. These are indeed relational definitions of *brahman.* Surely, they must not be construed to imply a transformation in the essential nature or *brahman* or a "climb down in the status of *brahman.*" Why are such definitions necessarily inferior? Creation does not introduce hitherto nonexistent distinctions in the nature of *brahman,* including the distinction of reality and appearance.

The problem and limits of language, it must be remembered, are also valid with reference to *brahman* as creator and in relation to the world. Here also, we must be conscious of the difference between the nature of *brahman* and the limits of our human ways of speaking about *brahman.* Human speech about *brahman,* even when such speech, because of the nature of language, seems to imply divisions in *brahman's* nature, does not, in actuality, create any divisions. To posit omnipotence as an attribute of *brahman,* for example, does not mean that *brahman* possess the attribute of omnipotence in the same way that a lotus has the color blue as its attribute. The act of creation and being in relation to the creation does not alter the unity of *brahman's* nature. The need to distinguish between a higher and lower *brahman* incorrectly underlines the fear of such a change.

If the nature of *brahman* is not two, and does not become two as a result of the creation of the world, we must question also the point of the distinction made between what is intrinsic or essential in the nature of *brahman* (*svarūpalakṣana*) and what is extrinsic or nonessential (*taṭasthalakṣana*).[16] Essential or intrinsic is equated with *nirguṇa* and nonessential or extrinsic with *saguṇa.* Creatorship and being in relation to the world are regarded as constituting the nonessential nature and definition of *brahman.* The essential nature of *brahman* is indicated by the words *satyam* (reality), *jñānam* (awareness), and *anantam* (infinite).[17] The terminology of essential and nonessential or intrinsic and extrinsic is as unfortunate as higher and lower since the nature of *brahman* does not admit of a division. The need for it arises from the concern, which we addressed earlier, that the attribution of creatorship to *brahman* is limiting and defective. The world is also devalued when it is regarded as the product of a nonessential nature of *brahman.* In any event, how could *brahman* possess nonessential characteristics if the basic distinction between substance and quality does not obtain?

The point that really ought to be made is that while *brahman* is the source, support, and end of the world, the world is dependent on *brahman* and not vice-versa. *Brahman* is *brahman* without the world, but the world is nonexistent without *brahman.* While *brahman* constitutes the essential nature of the world, the world does not constitute the essential nature of *brahman.* Although it is possible for us to speak in our limited language about *brahman* in relation to the world, neither our world nor our language limits *brahman.* If *saguṇa* reminds us that *brahman* is the sole source of our world, *nirguṇa* complements this truth by reminding us that the world does not limit or compromise *brahman's* nature. If *saguṇa* points to *brahman's* immanence, *nirguṇa* points to *brahman's* transcendence. These two terms should be seen, not as indicative of any hierarchy in the nature of *brahman,* but as necesary poles in the paradoxical language without which one cannot speak about *brahman.* They are complementary and not mutually exclusive ways of speaking, and superiority should not be accorded to the *nirguṇa* mode of discourse.

THE PROBLEM OF PURPOSE

Another significant reason for the denial of creatorship to *brahman,* the positing of *māyā* as the material cause of the world, the hierarchies of *nirguṇa* and *saguṇa*, and essential and nonessential natures is the difficulty of dealing with the purpose of creation. Why would the infinite *brahman,* without lack or want, engage in the act of creating the world? As Gauḍapāda states it in his *Kārika* (1.9) on the Māṇḍūkya Upaniṣad, "What desire can One have whose desire is ever fulfilled?"[18] Gauḍapāda deals with the problem of ascribing a motive to *brahman* by suggesting that creation is in the very nature of *brahman* (*devasya esaḥ svabhāvah ayam*).

In the *Brahmasūtra* (2.1.32), an argument is raised against *brahman* being the creator of the universe, and the problem of ascribing purpose to *brahman* is central to the issue. An intelligent being, argues the opponent, does not engage in activity without some self-purpose in view. If we attribute self-purpose to *brahman,* however, those Vedic texts that speak of *brahman's* limitlessness will be contradicted and, if purpose is denied, activity is impossible. It is true that a deranged person can act without purpose, but *brahman* is omniscient, and purposeless activity caused by derangement cannot be possible. The text responds to this objection by suggesting that the act of creation is the play (*līlā*) of *brahman.*[19] Śaṅkara explains the response by citing the example of a ruler.

> As in the world it is seen that though a king or some councilor of the king who has got all his desires fulfilled, may still, without any aim in view, indulge in activities in the forms of sports and pastimes, as a sort of diversion, or as inhalation, exhalation, etc., proceed spontaneously without depending on any external motive, so also God can have activities of the nature of mere pastime out of His spontaneity without any extraneous motive. For any motive imputed to God can have neither the support of the reason or of the Vedas.

Comans takes the position that the *Brahmasūtra* author preferred to render the creation rather pointless, instead of proposing "some inner need on the part of the Creator." He leaves this important subject acknowledging "the dilemma in understanding God's creation of the world."[20]

The predicament of *brahman* as a creator, for Advaita, is rooted in the view that purpose or desire signifies limitation and incompleteness. To avoid this, Gauḍapāda suggests that creation is an expression of the nature of *brahman.*[21] Although Śaṅkara concedes that some people may discern a subtle motive behind the *līlā* notion, he refutes this argument by falling back on the view that *brahman* has no unfullfilled desires.[22] This appears to be a concession by Śaṅkara that while *līlā* is not entirely disconnected from purpose, the purpose of *brahman* ought not to be equated with that of a limited being. He emphasizes that, for *brahman,* the act of creation is not one that involves the exercise of effort. It is brought into being with ease and spontaneity. One may venture to suggest also that Gauḍapāda was not denying purpose but emphasizing the ease and naturalness of the creative process and *brahman's* freedom from want. One wishes that both commentators had developed the argument further.

Unlike Advaita commentators, the Upaniṣads are not reticent about *brahman* as the creator and are not hesitant to suggest desire and purpose. Aitareya Upaniṣad (1.1), for example, begins with the act of creation.

> In the beginning this world was the self (*ātman*), one alone, and there was no other being at all that blinked an eye. He thought to himself: "Let me create the worlds."

In the Taittirīya Upaniṣad (2.6.1), the text not only identifies *brahman* as the creator of all, but also attributes to *brahman* the urge for self-multiplication and for birth.

> He (the Self wished), "Let me be many, let me be born," He undertook a deliberation. Having deliberated, he created all this that exists. That (*brahman*), having created (that), entered into that very thing. [23]

Chāndogya Upaniṣad (6.2.3) also mentions the desire of *brahman* for self-multiplication and birth.

> And it thought to itself: "Let me become many. Let me propagate myself."

The motive for creation most often mentioned in the Upaniṣads is the desire to become many (*bahu syām*) and we could speculate on what this might mean for a limitless being such as *brahman.* While positing a motive on the part of *brahman* for self-multiplication, the Upaniṣads do not suggest that such a motive indicates a lack or limit in *brahman.* A desire, in other words, is not necessarily incompatible with fullness of being and creation. Taittirīya Upaniṣad (3.6.1.) speaks of bliss as the origin, support, and end of all beings.[24]

> *Brahman* is bliss for, clearly, it is from bliss that these beings are born; through bliss, once born, do they live; and into bliss do they pass upon death.

It is meaningful that this Taittirīya text, when describing the origin of the world from *brahman,* chooses to do so with reference to the limitless bliss-nature (*ānanda*) of *brahman.* The suggestion is that creation is an outpouring of the fullness of *brahman* and not an act motivated by any sense of incompleteness. Actions springing from *ānanda* do not add to or diminish the fullness of *brahman*. Such actions may be construed as being celebrative in nature. The *Brahmasūtra* (2.1.33) uses the term *līlā* to suggest activity of this kind and Śaṅkara, as noted above, explains it through the analogy of sport or play. The point of the analogy, we want to suggest, is not to trivialize creation or liken the creativity of *brahman* to human diversion, but to indicate the possibility of action as celebrative self-expression and action that does not spring from self-limitation. This may be also Gauḍapadā's point in suggesting that the act of creation is in the very nature of *brahman*.[25] It is important to take note of the fact that Śaṅkara does admit the fact of desire on the part of *brahman*. He does this in Taittirīya Upaniṣad (2.6.1) in response to the argument that *brahman* is insentient.

> No, since It is capable of desiring. It is not certainly a matter of experience that one who can desire can be insentient. And we have said that *brahman* is, indeed omniscient; and so it is but reasonable that It should be capable of desiring.

The description of creation as *līlā* or self-expression, does not imply that *brahman* has no choice in the matter of creation or that there is not intentionality and will involved. *Brahman's* freedom must include the freedom to create or not to create. The effortlessness with which *brahman* creates should not be misread to mean that creation is not desired by *brahman* or that it is not a deliberate action. As the following argument reveals, this misunderstanding is still common.

> In the Upaniṣads, the universe is not distinct from *brahman* and is not brought into existence by an act of will. It is simply a manifestation or expression of *brahman's* being. The Muṇḍaka Upaniṣad compares the universe coming forth from *brahman* to various automatic, natural processes: "As plants grew from the soil and hair from the body of man, so springs the universe from the eternal *brahman*." The metaphor should not be pushed too hard, but it does accurately convey the sense that creation is not something planned, desired or willed by *brahman*.[26]

The intentionality of *brahman* in the act of creation is clearly indicated in the accounts, mentioned above, from the Aitareya, Chāndogya, and Taittirīya Upanisads. In the Aitareya (1.1) and Chāndogya (6.2.3), *brahman's* reflection/thought (*īkṣaṇa*) before creation is explicitly mentioned. Taittirīya (2.6.1) refers to *brahman's* desire to create (*so kāmayata*) and the process of deliberation/contemplation (*sa tapotapyata sa tapastaptva*) which precedes creation.[27] In his comment on *Brahmasūtra* (1.4.15) Śaṅkara specifically refutes any doctrine of spontaneous creation and underlines the role of *brahman* as creator.

> Besides, it can be understood that at the time of the first creation, the universe required some ordainer for its differentiation into names and forms, just

> as much as even today it has somebody to guide it when differentiating into names and forms (as pot, cloth, etc.) For any fancy that does not agree with observation is illogical. Moreover, another text, "Let me manifest name and form by Myself entering this as this individual soul" (CU.6.3.2) shows that the universe differentiated under some guidance.[28]

A similar argument is advanced in his commentary on Brahmasūtra (1.1.2).

> The origin of a world possessing the attributes stated above cannot possibly proceed from anything else but a Lord possessing the stated qualities; not either from a non-intelligent *pradhāna,* or from atoms, or from non-being, or from a being subject to transmigration; nor, again can it proceed from its own nature (i.e. spontenously, without a cause), since we observe that (for the production of effects) special places, times, and causes have invariably to be employed.[29]

Perhaps the most common example used by Advaita commentators to explain the nature of the creation is the rope-snake illustration.[30] A person walking along a path at dusk sees an object that he takes to be a snake. He is full of fear and apprehension, but approaches closer and realizes that the object is a piece of rope. His ignorance concealed the rope and projected a snake in its place. When the rope is discovered, the snake vanishes. In a similar way, one who is ignorant of *brahman* superimposes upon it the world of diversity. While the rope-snake example is helpful for explaining that the world does not have an existence and reality that is independent of *brahman,* and can be deceptive in presenting itself as ontologically independent, it is misleading in other aspects.

In a tradition for which the creatorship of *brahman* is problematic, the example is commonly used to point to the world as a product of the individual's ignorance, thus further disconnecting *brahman* from any involvement in the creative process.[31] The Upaniṣads, however, do not present the world as a projection of human ignorance. It is the deliberate creation of *brahman,* an outpouring of fullness. We experience a world of plurality, not as a consequence of our ignorance, but because such a world is willed into being by *brahman.* Ignorance causes us to misunderstand the nature of the world, but does not bring it into being. *Avidyā* (ignorance), we cannot emphasize enough, does not create the universe; it is responsible for a certain interpretation of its nature. Unlike the snake that is erroneously perceived in the place of a rope and then vanishes when the rope is discerned, one cannot think the world out of existence. Through knowledge, one understands the non-difference of the world from *brahman* and not its nonexistence. Since the world is not created by ignorance, it cannot be willed into nonexistence by knowledge. The change is only in our understanding of the nature of the world and our corresponding responses to it. This is a distinction that is not highlighted sufficiently in contemporary Advaita discourse. For Śaṅkara, as already noted above, the world has its source and origin in *brahman* alone and enjoys a reality that is independent of human thought. Yet Śaṅkara himself quite often speaks of the world as a product of ignorance (*avidyākṛta/avidyākalpita*), and in ways that are not always helpful in maintaining the distinction between ignorance as misunderstanding of reality and ignorance as cause of the world. The consequence of this is a negativization of creation as illustrated in his opening remarks on the Bṛhadāraṅyaka Upaniṣad linking the world as the creation of ignorance and the world as evil.

> This manifested universe, consisting of means and ends, was in an undifferentiated state before its manifestation. That relative universe, without beginning and end like the seed and the sprout etc., created by ignorance and consisting in a superimposition of action, its factors and its results on the Self, is an evil.[32]

The wish to become many (*bahu syām*) may also be thought of as an urge emanating from *brahman* to celebrate its being through self-replication. This is, admittedly, a desire, but not one that springs out of incompleteness.[33] In his commentary on Taittirīya Upaniṣad (2.6.1) Śaṅkara responds to the criticism that since *brahman* has desires, *brahman* also has wants like human beings.

> Not so, for It is independent. Such defects as desire cannot impel *brahman* to action, just as they do others, by subjecting them to their influence. What then are these (desires of *brahman*)? They are by nature truth and knowledge, and they are pure by virtue of their identity with *brahman*.[34]

Śaṅkara's point is that the desire of *brahman* proceeds out of the fullness of knowledge and not out of a sense of lack born from of ignorance. We may venture to suggest that Śaṅkara is more concerned with desire suggesting incompletness than desire per se. Actions born out of self-ignorance are performed with the desire to become a full being and are characterized by compulsiveness. They are motivated by a personal deficiency and want. The desire of *brahman* to become many ensues from the limitlessness (*ānanda*) of *brahman* and may be thought of as celebrative outpouring. It is expressive of the nature of *brahman* and not meant for the gain of something that would make *brahman,* in any sense, better. Desire is not inherently contradictory to the nature of *brahman,* as is often assumed in Advaita rhetoric.

Taittirīya Upaniṣad (2.6.1) and Chāndogya Upaniṣad (6.2.3) mention, in addition to *brahman's* desire to become many (*bahu syām*), the desire to be born (*prajāyeyeti*), which may also be translated as a desire for offspring. Praśna Upaniṣad (1.4) is more explicit and refers to the lord of beings as having a desire for progeny.[35] The wish for offspring may be construed as a desire on the part of *brahman* to share and celebrate its plenitude through self-multiplication. Since *brahman* is partless and indivisible, such self-multiplication means the creation of countless forms and *brahman* becoming the self of each one. Through *brahman's* existence as the self (*ātman*), all partake in the fullness of *brahman*. *Brahman's* self-sharing consists of giving its nature to all that is created by becoming the self of all. Human beings have the special privilege not only of participating in the fullness of *brahman,* but of knowing this liberating truth of the identity of *ātman* and *brahman.* Creation may be understood, therefore as the celebration of *brahman's* fullness through self-multiplication. In the case of human beings, it offers the possibility of participating in this celebration through knowing *brahman* as non-dual, the self of all, and as non-different from the world.

THE VALUE OF THE CREATION FOR *BRAHMAN*

The ineffability of *brahman* does not preclude us from suggesting that the creation has value for *brahman.* We have already noted Śaṅkara's unmistakable refutation, following the Upaniṣads, of the doctrine of spontaneous creation. Although conceding that the Upaniṣads offer varying accounts of the order of creation, he insists that "they have no difference as regards the Creator."[36] Creation accounts in the Upaniṣad also emphasize *brahman's* deliberation (*īkṣaṇa*) and intentionality before and during the process of creating. We must also take note of Śaṅkara's refutation of the possibility that *brahman's* act of creating may be likened to that of a deranged person who is without motive. This, according to Śaṅkara, is not possible since the scripture affirms both the fact of creation as well as the omniscience of *brahman.*[37]

Śaṅkara is also concerned to deny any suggestion that *brahman's* motives may be cruel or unjust. In *Brahmasūtra* 2.1.34, he responds to the argument that if *brahman* is the creator of the world, *brahman* "will be open to the charge of pitilessness and extreme cruelty, abhorred even by a villain." God, explains Śaṅkara, creates only in accordance with individual merit and demerit based on past lives.

> No fault attaches to God, since this unequal creation is brought about in conformity with the virtues and vices of the creatures that are about to be born. Rather, God is to be compared to rain. Just as rainfall is a common cause for the growth of paddy, barley, etc., the special reason for the differences being the individual potentiality of the respective seeds, similarly God is the common cause for the birth of gods, men and others, while the individual fruits of works associated with the individual creatures are the uncommon causes for the creation of the differences among the gods, men and others. Thus God is not open to the defects of partiality and cruelty, since He takes other factors into consideration.

To the argument that the fruits of action are operative only after creation, Śaṅkara takes recourse in the idea of a beginningless creation on the analogy of the seed and the sprout.[38] Śaṅkara's defense of *brahman* merits further discussion, but this is not our immediate concern. The important point here is his vigorous response to any suggestion that *brahman* is cruel or partial and his wish to affirm the essential goodness and justice of *brahman.*

All of the above reasons are adduced in support of our position that creation has value and significance for *brahman.* The doctrine of *līlā,* as already pointed out, should not be construed to mean frivolity. Its purpose is to avoid suggestions of limits in *brahman* and to underline the absence of effort and struggle in creation. The analogies, used by Śaṅkara and other Advaitins, that liken *brahman* to a magician and the world to a magical illusion are quite unfortunate.[39] While the underlying intention is to emphasize the ontological non-dualism and dependent reality of the creation, as well as the transcendence of the creator, these analogies, by their repetitiveness and suggestion of an intent to deceive, in the absence of alternative analogies trivialize creation and do not propose any positive worth that it may have for the creator. Today, new analogies are needed. A creation that is presented as bereft of value to the creator cannot have value for the created. We must admit that Śaṅkara himself, though arguing forcefully for *brahman* as creator and refuting the subjectivism of certain Buddhist schools, is not always consistent in this position and frequently uses examples that are more meaningfully employed in articulating a subjective idealist position

While being cognizant of the limits of reasoning and the inadequacies of analogies, it is not impossible, with the aid of the Upaniṣads, to glimpse the significance of *brahman's* desire to share its plenitude through self-multiplication.[40] The desire for meaning, as numerous personal stories in the Upaniṣads reveal, is fundamental to the human being.[41] The meaning of human existence, however, cannot be understood apart from the purpose of the one who brought all things into being. The Upaniṣads do not present *brahman* as non-involved in the creation of the world or as without intentionality and purpose, although many interpreters labor to do so. If one sees the world as a projection or superimposition on *brahman* wrought by ignorance (*avidyā*), like the snake on a rope, one's attitude to the world is correspondingly negative, since its negation is necessary for the gain of *brahman.* There is an emphasis on world-renunciation. If the world, on the other hand, is seen positively as the outcome of the intentional creativity of *brahman,* expressing and sharing the fullness of *brahman,* the world does not have to be negated or rejected. The purpose of human life, then, is to participate in the celebration of existence by knowing the nature of the one who has brought all things into being, whose nature infuses everything and whose fullness we share.

CHAPTER SEVEN

Liberation

The fundamental human problem, articulated in Advaita, is self-ignorance. The existence of the self (*ātman*) does not have to be established by the use of any means of valid knowledge (*pramāṇa*) since the self, as awareness, is self-revealed. The existence of the self is implied in every act of thinking, even in the act of doubting the existence of the self. "Every effort to disprove the existence of the self," writes T. W. Organ, "established the self, because the transcendent condition of knowledge is presupposed in the very act of refutation."[1] "The Self," writes Śaṅkara, "is not absolutely beyond apprehension, because It is apprehended as the content of the concept 'I' and because the Self, opposed to the non-Self, is well known as an immediately perceived (i.e. self-revealing) entity."[2] Since one is not separated from one's self by time or space, temporal and spatial divisions do not have to be bridged for the purposes of attaining the self. The self is always here and now.

THE NATURE OF IGNORANCE

Although self-revealing and immediately available as the content of the "I" thought, the specific nature of the self remains unknown. It is the nature of the self and not its existence that is the subject of ignorance. The search is to know "*what* it is, not *that* it is."[3] Ignorance of the specific nature of the self causes one to fully and incorrectly identify the self with the attributes of the body, senses, and mind and to superimpose the finitude of these upon the self. The self is then regarded as a limited entity that is bound by time and space and subject to bodily characteristics such as birth, growth, change, decline, and death. Mental and emotional states such as anger and desire are also identified with the self. Erroneous conclusions about the self, however, do not bring about any change or transformation in its actual nature. Misapprehending the nature of the self and identifying it with the non-self do not make it a limited, wanting, and mortal entity. The nature of the self is not affected by what one thinks of it.

The proposition of ignorance (*avidyā*) as the fundamental human problem is not intended to deny or trivialize the reality of human suffering. Ignorance does not imply that suffering is nonexistent and ought not to be taken seriously. The intent here is to identify ignorance of the nature of the self as a foundational error that is a primary cause of human suffering. Ignorance of the limitless self is the original cause of the sense of want and inadequacy experienced by the human being. This leads to greed (*kāma*) or the multiplication of desires in an effort to assuage the condition of incompleteness. The realization of desires for objects other than the self results in a short-lived fulfillment that leaves the basic condition of human inadequacy, and the suffering it engenders, unresolved. When greed, born of *avidyā,* expresses itself in behavior that is indifferent to the well-being of others, it becomes socially harmful and destructive. It is unfortunate that the orientation of the Advaita tradition to individual liberation has resulted in minimal attention to the social consequences of *avidyā.* There is much that the traditon can contribute here to our understanding of the psychological roots of oppression and injustice, but such an analysis presupposes a greater value for life in the world. While retaining its focus on liberation (*mokṣa*), there are good reasons why the insights of the Advaita tradition ought to be creatively employed to understand and suggest solutions for human socioeconomic and political problems.

Ignorance of the self, and consequent identification with the non-self, are also at the root of our fears and anxieties about aging and dying. In seeking to understand the sources of human suffering, Advaita calls attention to its epistemological or psychological roots in false assumptions about the self. Although the self, as non-different from the limitless *brahman,* is full, immortal and not subject to the ravages of time, ignorance brings about suffering by engendering feelings of inadequacy, fear, and anxiety. *Avidyā* is the original error and the first link in the well-known causal chain (*avidyā-kāma-karma*) leading to human suffering. Its removal, therefore, is the *sine qua non* for human well-being.

LIBERATION AS IDENTICAL WITH THE NATURE OF *BRAHMAN*

Liberation (*mokṣa*) in Advaita is identical with the nature of the self, and since the self does not have to be attained, *mokṣa* is already and always accomplished. "The cessation of ignorance alone," says Śaṅkara, "is commonly called liberation."[4] The gain or attainment of *mokṣa* is meaningful only with reference to the removal of false conclusions about the nature of the self. If *mokṣa* is conceived of as a nonexistent condition brought into being through actions of some kind, it would be noneternal like all created things. Śaṅkara's extensive commentary on Brahmasūtra (1.1.4) is concerned, almost entirely, with establishing that liberation is synonymous with the nature of the self and thus already attained and eternal. He argues this point from a variety of perspectives.

> Therefore, there can be no question of liberation becoming impermanent, for in it is revealed the reality of the eternally free Self, after eliminating from the Self the idea of Its being under the bondage (of birth and death), fancied on It through ignorance. But from the standpoint of one who believes that liberation is a product, it is but logical that there should be a dependence on activity—mental, vocal and physical. The position becomes the same if liberation be a transformation of something. From either point of view, liberation must of necessity be impermanent; for neither curd that is a modification, nor a jar that is a product is seen to be permanent in this world. And no dependence on work can be proved by assuming liberation to be a thing to be acquired; for it being essentially one with one's very Self, there can be no acquisition. . . . Liberation cannot also be had through purification, so as to be dependent on action. Purification is achieved either through the addition of some quality or the removal of some defect. As to that, purification is not possible here through the addition of any quality, since liberation is of the very nature of *brahman* on which no excellence (or deterioration) can be effected. Nor is that possible through the removal of any defect, for liberation is of the very nature of *brahman* that is ever pure.[5]

Bondage, for Śaṅkara, is essentially an erroneous idea (*bhrānti*) in the mind, and liberation is its removal. Liberation is not a change in the state or nature of the *ātman.* The conditions of ignorance or knowledge in the mind do not imply change in the self. The change implied in the gain of liberation is really the loss of ignorance. "To be liberated is *to know* oneself and *to be* what one really is. It is not *to do* or *to become* something."[6]

> Really there is no such distinction as liberation and bondage in the self, for it is eternally the same; but the ignorance regarding it is removed by the knowledge arising from the teachings of the scriptures, and prior to the receiving of these teachings, the effort to attain liberation is perfectly reasonable.[7]

EMBODIED OR LIVING LIBERATION

The identification of liberation with the nature of the self which is already and always attained and the emphasis on the removal of ignorance in the mind lead logically to the view that liberation is possible here and now. It is not an end that must await the death of the body since ignorance is not synonymous with the fact of the self's association with a body, but with the erroneous identification of the self and the body. It is not the absence of a body that constitutes liberation, but the elimination of ignorance about the nature of the self. The state of embodied or living liberation is referred to as *jīvanmukti*, and the liberated person is called a *jīvanmukta.*[8]

Śaṅkara clearly supports embodied liberation. In his remarks on Kaṭha Upaniṣad (2.2.2), for example, he comments on the fearlessness of the liberated person. "How can there be any vision of fear, since there is no occasion for sorrow after the attainment of fearlessness from His realisation? Even here, (while still living), he becomes *vimuktaḥ,* free."[9] He interprets Kaṭha Upaniṣad (2.3.4), ("He attains *brahman* here") to mean the discovery of one's identity with *brahman* while living and emphasizes that "here alone is it possible for the vision of the Self to be as clear as a mirror."[10] Like a snake casting off its old skin, the liberated person ceases to identify the self with the body. Though still associated with a mortal body, the liberated, through wisdom, is bodiless and immortal.

> Because formerly he was embodied and mortal on account of his identification with the body under the influence of his desires and past work; since that is gone, he is now disembodied, *and* therefore *immortal.*[11]

While *mokṣa* is understood primarily as freedom from self-ignorance which is to be attained here and now, ignorance leads to assumptions about oneself and attitudes toward others that result in unhappiness and suffering (*duḥkha*). *Mokṣa,* therefore, may also be understood as freedom from all *avidyā*-generated conditions that cause suffering. Foremost among these is desire, a direct consequence of ignorance.

LIBERATION AS FREEDOM FROM DESIRE

The Upaniṣads consistently describe the liberated person as one who is free from desire. Muṇḍaka Upaniṣad (3.2.1) speaks of such a person as being free from desire here itself (*ihaiva sarve pravilīyanti kāmāḥ*). Kaṭha Upaniṣad (2.3.14) identifies the gain of liberation and immortality with the shedding of desires. Bhagavadgītā (2:71) speaks of the liberated person as abandoning all desires (*vihāya kāmān yaḥ sarvān*). *Avidyā* generates desires because it causes a false sense of incompleteness and inadequacy consequent on taking the self to be what it is not. The self (*ātman*), which is not different in its essential nature from the infinite (*brahman*), is taken to be deficient and incomplete. Desires of various kinds are then entertained in order to achieve completeness and self-value. The fulfillment of such desires, however, results only in momentary experiences of completeness, and new desires are soon generated. One becomes, in the words of the Bhagavadgītā (2:70), a desirer of objects (*kāmakāmi*).

The liberation from desire, about which the Upaniṣads speak so eloquently, is the result of the discovery of the self to be full and complete. The connection between the discovery of the fullness of the self and freedom from desires is most explicit in Kṛṣṇa's definition of the person with wisdom in the Bhagavadgītā (2:55). In 2:54, Arjuna requested a description of the person whose knowledge of the self is firmly established (*sthitaprajña*). Arjuna's curiosity, however, appears to be centered on the externally identifiable behavior characteristics of the liberated person. He inquires about the person's mode of speaking, sitting and moving around. In his response, Kṛṣṇa ignores the specifics of Arjuna's question and speaks of the fullness of the self and freedom from desire.

> When one drops all desires generated in the mind and is contented in the self, by the self, one is called a person of steady knowledge.[12]

It is the understanding of the fullness of the self that makes the release from the grip of desire possible. A contentment that is the result of self-knowledge does not depend on the fulfilment or nonfulfilment of desires. It is centered on the nature of the self that is not subject to change, and hence is not momentary.

LIBERATION AS THE ATTAINMENT OF FULLNESS OF SELF

The positive side of the liberation from desire, which is implied in the gain of *mokṣa,* is the attainment of fullness of self. The state of fullness that a person seeks vainly through the multiplication of desires for objects and pleasures is found in the nature of the self. The Upaniṣads make this point often by describing the knowledge of self as resulting in the fulfillment or attainment of all desires. In Taittirīya Upaniṣad (2.1.1) the knower of *brahman,* which is truth, knowledge, and infinite (*satyam jñānamanantam*), is said to attain all desires (*so 'śnute sarvān kāmān saha*).[13] In the Chāndogya Upaniṣad (8.7.1–8.13), two students, Indra and Virochana, approach the teacher, Prajāpati, with the request for the knowledge of the self that leads to the attainment of all worlds and desires.

The attainment of the self is attainment of happiness, since happiness constitutes the very nature of *brahman.* When Bhṛgu, in Taittirīya Upaniṣad (3.6.1), finally understood the nature of *brahman,* he understood it as the bliss from which all things are born, by which they are sustained and into which they return. Commenting on this verse, Śaṅkara explains that one who comes to know *brahman* as bliss "gets similarly fixed in the bliss that is the supreme *brahman;* that is to say, he becomes *brahman* itself." Taittirīya Upaniṣad (2.9.1) relates the discovery of the bliss that is *brahman* with the realization of fearlessness.[14] "*Brahman,*" states Bṛhadāraṇyaka Upaniṣad (4.3.32), "is supreme bliss. On a particle of this bliss do other creatures live." In the Chāndogya Upaniṣad (7.1.3) Nārada goes to his teacher, Sanatkumāra, for knowledge of the self that frees from sorrow (*tarati śokamātmavit*) and learns that the infinite alone is bliss. There is no bliss in the finite.

Liberation from desire is equated, especially in the Bhagavadgītā, with the attainment of peace (*śānti*). It is the person who overcomes desires and not the one who is the victim of desires who obtains peace (2:70–71). The attainment of knowledge is possible for the person who has faith (*śraddha*) and the consequence of knowledge is the speedy realization of supreme peace (4:39). Kaṭha Upaniṣad (1.3.13) speaks of the self as peaceful (*śānta*) and of eternal peace only for those who discover the self within (2.2.13). Taittirīya Upaniṣad (1.6.2) identifies peace as the very nature of the self (*śānti samṛddham*), reminding us that peace is not to be understood as an attribute of the self. Peace is the self which is full and free.

LIBERATION AS FREEDOM FROM MORTALITY

Mokṣa is liberation from mortality and the fear of death. Positively expressed, it is the attainment of immortality. Overcoming the fear of death and attaining immortality are the meanings of *mokṣa* most often noted in the Upaniṣads. Mortality and the attendant fear of death are the consequences of wrongly identifying the self with the mortal body. The attainment of immortality is not achieved through transformation into immortality of that which is, by nature, mortal. Immortality is the very nature of the self and the attainment of immortality, spoken of in the Upaniṣads, is elimination of ignorance which causes one to consider the self to be mortal. Kena Upaniṣad (2.4) speaks of the attainment of immortality through knowledge (*vidyayā vindate 'mṛtam*). Through knowledge one can attain only that which is already attained, and the attainment of the self, as has been noted throughout, is of this kind. The famous Muṇḍaka Upaniṣad (3.2.9) affirmation, "The knower of *brahman* becomes *brahman* (*brahma veda brahmaiva bhavati*)," does not indicate a process of becoming. One becomes *brahman* through knowledge only because the self is *brahman* and one attains immortality because it is the nature of the self.

Immortality is not achieved by or equated with a journey into a heavenly world. Since liberation, which is the nature of the self, is attained here, so also is immortality. Bṛhadāraṇyaka Upaniṣad (4.4.7) speaks of attaining immortality in this world. While conceding that the word *svarga* is generally used to indicate a heavenly region or place, Śaṅkara notes that there are contexts when *svarga* refers to *mokṣa*.[15] Commenting on the reference to *svarge loke* in Kena Upaniṣad, Śaṅkara interprets it as referring to *brahman* who is all bliss. Being qualified by the words *ananta* (infinite) and *jyeye* (highest), *svarga* does not refer to heaven, but to the self that is infinite and higher than all else.

> Lest the word boundless (*ananta*) be taken in any secondary sense, the text says *jyeye*, in the higher, that which is greater than all, in one's own Self which is boundless in the primary sense. The purport is that he does not again return to this world.[16]

LIBERATION AS FREEDOM FROM THE CYCLES OF REBIRTH

Implied in the attainment, through knowledge, of the self which is immortal, is liberation from the cycles of rebirth and redeath (*saṁsāra*). There is no journey after death for one who knows the non-difference of the self and *brahman*. Liberated in life with a body (*jīvanmukti*), such a person is also liberated after death without a body (*videhamukti*). Bṛhadāraṇyaka Upaniṣad (4.4.6–7) offers a description of this liberation.

> Of him who is without desires, who is free from desires, the objects of whose desire have been attained, and to whom all objects of desire are but the Self—the organs do not depart. Being but *brahman,* he is merged in *brahman.*
>
> Regarding this there is this verse: "When all the desires that dwell in his heart are gone, then he, having been mortal, becomes immortal, and attains *brahman* in this very body." Just as the lifeless slough of a snake is cast off and lies in the ant-hill, so does this body lie. Then the self becomes disembodied and immortal, becomes the Supreme Self, *brahman,* the Light.[17]

The non-departure of the organs, indicated above, speaks of what we referred to earlier as the subtle body (*sūkṣma śarīra*).[18] In the case of a person who is not liberated, death implies the disintegration of the physical body (*sthūla śarīra*). The subtle body, enlivened by the conscious self, and in accordance with its actions and desires, eventually gets associated with a new physical body. While the physical body is changed in each new birth, the subtle body endures until liberation.[19] The continuity of the individual person (*jīva*) is preserved from birth to birth through the persistence of the subtle body.[20] The end of self-ignorance, which is the same as the gain of liberation, results in freedom from desire. There are now no personal unfulfilled desires, instigated by self-ignorance, to necessitate rebirth.[21] The subtle body, without the impetus of desire, does not depart. Like the physical body, it reverts to the subtle elements, and the limitless self abides in its own nature. Śaṅkara compares it to a wave attaining identity with the ocean.[22] Muṇḍaka Upaniṣad (3.2.8) uses a striking image to describe the state of liberation.

> As rivers, flowing down, become indistinguishable on reaching the sea by giving up their names and forms, so also the illumined soul, having become freed from name and form, reaches the self-effulgent Puruṣa that is higher than the higher.

Śaṅkara, in his commentary on the Muṇḍaka Upaniṣad, cites the Māhābhārata text, "Just as the footmarks of birds cannot be traced in the sky or of fish in the water, so is the departure of the illumined." The attainment of *brahman* by the liberated, writes Śaṅkara, is not at all like a journey to a location in space. Only a limited object can be attained by such a journey.

> *Brahman,* being the All, is not to be approached through spatial limitations. Should *brahman* be circumscribed by space like any concrete object, It will also have a beginning and an end. It will be supported by something else, It will have parts and It will be impermanent and a product. But *brahman* cannot be so; therefore Its attainment, too, cannot be determined in terms of the limitation of space. Besides, the knowers of *brahman* accept only that liberation which consists in the removal of ignorance etc., and not that which is a product.[23]

LIBERATION AS FREEDOM FROM *KARMA*

Liberation from the cycle of rebirth and redeath also implies freedom from *karma*, or the fruits of action. "When that Self," states Muṇḍaka Upaniṣad (2.2.8), "which is both high and low, is known, the knots of the heart get untied, all doubts become solved and all one's actions become dissipated." It is the necessity to experience the fruits of action, instigated by desire and rooted in ignorance, that perpetuates the cyle of rebirth. Śaṅkara uses the familiar triad *avidyā-kāma-karma* (ignorance-desire-action), at various points in his commentaries, to illustrate the relationships in this causal chain.[24]

In the Advaita tradition, the fruits of actions are described as being threefold. The first is *sañcita karma,* the accumulated or stored-up effects of past actions that are yet to produce results. The second is *āgamī karma,* the effects of actions that are being done in the current life and which will bear fruit in the future. The third is *prārabdha karma,* the effects of past actions that are already bearing fruit in the present life. The knowledge of the self's non-difference from *brahman* destroys the accumulated effects of past actions that are yet to produce results. The actions that are done by the liberated person in the current life, after the gain of self-knowledge, do not generate results that necessitate rebirth since they are done without egotistic desire for personal gain and with an understanding of the *ātman's* difference from the body, mind, and ego. One no longer identifies oneself as a limited doer and enjoyer.[25] The results of actions that are the cause of the present life and are bearing fruit continue to do so and, upon their exhaustion, bodily death occurs. Like an arrow discharged from a bow, which cannot be recalled, or a potter's wheel that maintains its momentum, *prārabdha karma* is responsible for the continuity of bodily existence for the liberated. As a consequence of self-knowledge, however, the liberated one does not identify the self with the body.

Śaṅkara clearly argues for the elimination of *sañcita* and *āgamī karmas* by knowledge and the continuity of *prārabdha karma* until death. Commenting on *Brahmasūtra,* Śaṅkara writes that "after the acquisition of knowledge, those virtues and vices that have not begun to yield their fruits and that were accumulated in earlier lives or even in this life before the dawn of knowledge are alone destroyed, but not so are those destroyed whose results have been partially enjoyed and by which has begun this present life in which the knowledge of *brahman* arises."[26] In response to the opponent's argument that it is contradictory for knowledge to destroy only some and not all forms of *karma,* Śaṅkara points out that a body is required for the acquisition of knowledge and the body is a product of *karma* which must run its course like the wheel of a potter. The testimony of the *jīvanmukta* is additional evidence for the continuity of the body after liberation. "For when somebody feels in his heart that he has realized *brahman* and yet holds the body, how can this be denied by somebody else?"[27]

While it is generally accepted that liberation with a body (*jīvanmukti*) results, after death, in the state of liberation without a body (*videhamukti*) and freedom from the cycle of rebirth, Śaṅkara, following *Brahmasūtra* (3.3.32), "Those who have a mission to fulfill continue in the corporeal state as long as the mission demands it (*yāvadadhikāramavasthitirādhikarikaṇām*)," accepts the possibility of rebirth for the liberated. Such a rebirth occurs when the liberated one is entrusted by God with a special mission (*adhikāra*), such as the propagation of the scriptures, and continues until the specific mission is accomplished. With the accomplishment of their missions, such persons are freed from further rebirth. This argument of the *Brahmasūtra,* supported by Śaṅkara, is an interesting one, for it suggests that although liberation from the cycle of rebirth and redeath is the consequence of the self-knowledge, the will of *brahman* is supreme and may occasionally intervene and alter the normal connection between knowledge and freedom from rebirth. It also supports the view that the impediment to liberation is not the body, but ignorance about the self.

LIBERATION AS FREEDOM IN ACTION

In the knots of the heart triad, *avidyā* (ignorance)-*kāma* (desire)-*karma* (action), the removal of ignorance through knowledge of the self results also in freedom from desire and action. It is extremely important to emphasize that the desires and actions from which one is liberated are those that, as the triad suggests, are generated by ignorance of the self. Such desires are instigated by the assumption that the self is incomplete and they lead to actions that are meant for the achievement of completeness and adequacy of self. Since the original conclusion about the self, according to Advaita, is false, desires and actions that follow from it will not produce fullness of self. When the nature of the self is known, desires prompted by ignorance are no longer entertained and pursued. This should not be construed to mean that the liberated person is incapable of desiring and performing actions in the world. The freedom of the liberated one surely includes the freedom to desire and act in ways that express the truth of the self. Even as *avidyā* is not the mere fact of having a body, but identifying the body with the self, *avidyā* cannot also be equated with desiring and doing actions. Just as the body ceases to be an impediment when there is self-knowledge, desires and actions that are expressive of ignorance also come to an end. The liberated one is now free to entertain desires and engage in actions that express a new understanding of self.

Although the Upaniṣads, because of veneration and regard for the *jīvanmukta* and her state of freedom, do not prescribe any obligatory actions, there is nothing inherent in the liberated state that makes actions for the well-being and happiness of others impossible. On the contrary, the understanding of the non-dual self that is synonymous with the attainment of liberation provides a powerful justification and impetus for a life of compassion and service. The freedom from *avidyā*-born desires does not destroy every motivation for action. The shedding of egotistic desires liberates one to work for others. This is the point of Kṛṣṇa's argument in the third chapter (22–24) of the

Bhagavadgītā. Using himself as an example of a liberated being with no personal ends to accomplish, he emphasizes that he still engages in action for the well-being of the world. In a similar way, argues Kṛṣṇa, the liberated one, free from selfish attachment, can work for the welfare of the world (*lokasaṁgraha*). In fact, Kṛṣṇa seems to suggest (3:25) that the liberated can bring the same energy and enthusiasm to working for others that an unliberated person brings to the pursuit of personal ends. Śaṅkara concurs with Kṛṣṇa's view in this discussion that actions for others are possible in the absence of personal desires. He understands Kṛṣṇa, in these verses, to be speaking about the knower of the self and paraphrases Kṛṣṇa's meaning in 3:25 as follows: "For Me, or for any other person who, knowing the Self, thus seeks the welfare of the world, there is nothing to do except it be with a view to that welfare of the world at large."[28]

The Bhagavadgītā, on two occasions (5:25;12:4) uses the expression "delighting in the welfare of all (*sarvabhūtahite ratāḥ*)" to describe the attitude of the liberated toward all beings. Although Śaṅkara does not elaborate on this phrase and although "delighting in the welfare of all" could be construed quite passively, there is no good reason why it ought to be. Kṛṣṇa was earlier (3:22–24) speaking clearly about and offering himself as an example of an active effort on behalf of others and contending that one has a responsibility (3:26) to set an example of right action.

Admittedly, both the Bhagavadgītā and Śaṅkara express *lokasaṁgraha* in rather limited ways. Kṛṣṇa speaks of his inaction as resulting in a mixture of castes, and Śaṅkara refers to the *jīvanmukta* as a teacher. In his commentary on Chāndogya Upaniṣad (6.14.2), he discusses the teacher as a liberated being who teaches because of his compassion for the suffering of the student. From the side of the teacher, it is "imperative that he should save from the ocean of ignorance any good disciple that approaches him duly."[29] Śaṅkara's emphasis on the teaching role of the *jīvanmukta* ought to be seen in the light of the Advaita emphasis on self-ignorance as the root of suffering and on the assumption that *jīvanmuktas* are few in number. The qualified and effective teacher is one who knows the Vedas and who is established personally in its teachings. If the *jīvanmukta* is motivated to teach because of compassion for the suffering student and a desire to set her free, there is no good reason why other kinds of actions, similarly motivated by compassion for the suffering of others, are not possible. The kinds of activites in which a liberated person may engage do not have to be narrowly construed, and the Advaita understanding of liberation, as formulated in this discussion, is entirely consistent with this understanding. While it is true that the involvement of the *jīvanmukta* in activities that go beyond teaching is not a traditional position, the question today is whether such involvement is desirable and if the Advaita understanding of liberation allows for it. This study is affirmative on both questions. Unfortunately, the tradition of *sannyāsa* associated with Advaita has led to an emphasis on the renunciation of action and this seems to be the emphasis in the commentaries of Śaṅkara. For Śaṅkara, the knowledge of *brahman* leads naturally to *sannyāsa* and renunciation, and this position, I believe, along with the failure to attribute value to the world, has not encouraged efforts to articulate reasons for positive engagement in the world.[30]

Śaṅkara has a limited perspective when he speaks about desire and action in relation to human motivation. He consistently identifies desires with the yearning for wife, sons, wealth, and other worlds. Since the knowledge of one's identity with *brahman* is supposed to remove such desires, renunciation naturally follows and the renunciant engages in minimal action for the maintenence of the physical body.[31] There is no need also to perform ritual actions that have these goals in view.[32] The consequence is an emphasis on withdrawal from activity on the part of the knower of *brahman* and an absence of interest in considering motives for action that are not limited to those identified by Śaṅkara. Although he admits, following the Bhagavadgītā, that the liberated person can engage in actions for the welfare of the world, this is not a viewpoint that he articulates anywhere else. It is fair to say that action in the world has generally negative connotations in the interpretations of Śaṅkara, and these are not commended with enthusiasm. His understanding and concern with human suffering is largely individual in nature and focused on the removal of self-ignorance.

LIBERATION AS IDENTIFICATION WITH ALL BEINGS

The liberating knowledge of the self, in Advaita, includes the understanding that the self is the self of all. The knower of the self, according to Bhagavadgītā (6:29), sees the self in all beings and all beings in the self. Īśa Upaniṣad (6–7) relates the knowedge of the oneness of the self to freedom from hate, delusion, and sorrow.

> One who sees all beings in the self alone and the self in all beings, feels no hatred by virtue of that understanding.
>
> For the seer of oneness, who knows all beings to be the self, where is delusion and sorrow?[33]

The knowledge of the indivisibility of the self, properly understood, leads to a deeper identity and affinity with all. Liberation does not alienate, isolate, or separate one from the community of other beings but awakens one to the truth of life's unity and interrelatedness. The value that one discovers for oneself when one understands one's true nature as non-different from *brahman* is a value that extends to and includes all beings.

While the Upaniṣads and the classical Advaita tradition do not pursue the implications of this understanding for the life of the *jīvanmukta* in society, there is no reason why we should not do so today. In the Bhagavadgītā, the discussion on the identity of the self in all is followed by a verse (6:32) that praises the highest *yogī* as the one who, because of knowing the truth of the self, owns the pain and suffering of others as his own. The result of self-knowledge, in other words, is an empathetic way of being. In his comment on this verse, Śaṅkara writes that this person "sees that whatever is pleasant to himself is pleasant to all creatures and whatever is painful to himself is painful to all beings. Thus seeing that what is pleasure or pain to himself is alike pleasure and pain to all beings, he causes pain to no being; he is harmless. Doing no harm and devoted to right knowledge, he is regarded as the highest among all *yogins*."[34]

Śaṅkara's comments on Bhagavadgītā (6:32) and Īśa Upaniṣad (6) emphasize freedom from hate and abstention from causing harm to others rather than compassion and engagement in action for the alleviation of suffering. The implications of the truth of self-knowledge are interpreted passively. If the knowledge of the non-duality of self results, as the Bhagavadgītā (6:32) puts it, in seeing the suffering of another as one's own, undertaking actions for the alleviation of suffering becomes a necessary outcome. Seeing the suffering of the other as one's own suffering becomes rather meaningless if this insight does not instigate action to help the other. Although suffering is ultimately rooted in *avidyā,* and a *jīvanmukta* may choose to focus her energies on teaching, this should not be seen as the only possible or legitimate activity for the liberated person and the Advaita tradition has to accommodate a variety of liberated lifestyles.

While recognizing *avidyā* to be the fundamental cause of suffering, Advaita must not ignore the suffering of human beings when they lack opportunities to attain the necessities for decent living such as food, housing, clean water, health care, and literacy or when suffering is inflicted through injustice and oppression based on gender, caste, or race. Such forms of suffering are not to be disconnected from the concern with *mokṣa.* Human beings subject to such deprivation often lack the resources that are congenial to the quest for liberation. We need, in other words, to question and detail the meaning of the ideal of *mokṣa* for just social, economic, and political relationships. It is not acceptable to affirm truths about the non-duality of the self and discerning one's self in all while being indifferent to the gross indignities and inequalities at the social level. The Advaita tradition has not been a strong advocate, as it could be, for justice. Andrew Fort is correct in his observation that "traditional Advaitins find the highest non-dual truth irrelevant to equality in everyday social relations."[35]

The vision of the self in all beings is articulated in the Upaniṣads as an outcome of *brahmajñāna* in the expectation that such a perspective enriches and enhances the meaning of being human and will be warmly embraced as a truth that enables us to overcome alienation and estrangement. The response to seeing oneself in another is love. It makes it possible for us to identify with others beyond the boundaries of our nationality, ethnicity, tribe, religion, and culture, to share their suffering and rejoice in their well-being. It challenges attitudes of uncaring indifference toward the suffering of others with whom we do not normally identify. It enables us to see living beings as constituting a single community and provides a philosophical basis for a compassionate and inclusive community where the worth and dignity of every human being is affirmed and where justice, at all levels, is sought. This will not occur, however, until the Advaita tradition positively asserts the value of the world and human existence within it, the necessity of reconciling religious insight and social reality, and the importance of working to transform the latter in the light of the former.

While agreeing with Fort that traditional Advaita has not concerned itself with equality in the social sphere, it must be added that there are no insurmountable philosophical reasons for this indifference and many more good ones exist that would justify such concern and action. In addition to the reasons noted above, it is important to remind ourselves that knowing *brahman* and attaining liberation do not imply that the world ceases to exist for the liberated. The world exists for both the person who knows *brahman* and the person who does not know *brahman.* The difference is that the knower of *brahman* understands the world to be an expression of *brahman* and to be dependent on *brahman* for its existence and reality.[36] Since ultimate reality and value belong to *brahman,* the world, as a celebrative expression of the plenitude of *brahman* and as partaking of the nature of *brahman,* has significance and worth. There is no need, as some Advaita commentators do, to devalue or negate the world in order to affirm the value of *brahman.*

The distinction, in terms of the experience of the world, between the liberated and the unliberated is understanding or not understanding the world in its relation to *brahman.* It is reasonable to assume that the liberated person who sees the world in relation to *brahman,* and who knows the fullness of the self and its indivisibility in all beings, will also see the suffering that human beings inflict on each other and on themselves when they are ignorant of the truth of *brahman.* The experience of liberation, which expresses itself in compassion, concern for others, and a desire to share one's liberative understanding, provides the motivation for offering an alternative vision of what the world could be if human relationships and social structures express the truth of *brahman.* These are the sources that also provide a basis for critiquing structures and relationships that reveal ignorance of *brahman* and which result in suffering and divisiveness. If *brahman's* self-multiplication is understood to be celebrative, participation in this celebration requires understanding of the truth of *brahman's* nature. Such an interpretation, while not historically prominent in Advaita, is fully consistent with its worldview and its understanding of the nature of liberation.

LIBERATION AS KNOWING *BRAHMAN* TO BE SELF AND GOD

Advaita writers who make a sharp distincton between *brahman* as *saguṇa* and *brahman* as *nirguṇa* commonly argue that the understanding of *brahman* as *saguṇa* is a mere stepping-stone on the path to liberation. Only the knowledge of *brahman* as *nirguṇa* constitutes liberative knowledge. *Saguṇa brahman* is *brahman* thought of as cause, creator, and sustainer of the universe, while *nirguṇa brahman* is *brahman* without any relation to the universe.

> It is God as Saguṇa-Brahman that is endowed with such qualities as love, kindness, mercy. Saguṇa-Brahman is personal God. But since qualities and relations can only belong in the realm of appearances, Saguṇa-Brahman is God as appearance and not as reality. On the other hand, Nirguṇa-Brahman, being reality beyond names and forms, is neither the cause nor the creator nor the sustainer nor the destroyer of the universe. God as Nirguṇa-Brahman can be neither worshipped nor prayed to. God as Nirguṇa-Brahman is Pure Being, Pure Consciousness and Pure Bliss.[37]

The argument that liberation requires the transcendence of *saguṇa-brahman* for *nirguṇa-brahman* is based, of course on the questionable bifurcation of *brahman's* nature which was questioned earlier.[38] It also connected with the viewpoint that attributes ontological status to *māyā* as the material cause of the world.[39] *Brahman,* by itself, it is argued, is incapable of creating anything. In association with *māyā*, *brahman* becomes capable of creating, preserving, and withdrawing the universe. *Brahman,* as associated with *māyā,* however, is the "lower" *brahman,* referred to as *īśvara* or *saguṇa-brahman. Īśvara* is not *brahman* in *brahman's* ultimate nature, for it is God as person, and *īśvara* only has the same degree of reality as *māyā*. Liberation, in this view, "is to go beyond Īśvara, to know the impersonal Reality behind the personal divine Appearance."[40]

Since this study has questioned the hierarchical distinction between *brahman* as *saguṇa* and *brahman* as *nirguṇa* as well as the ontological status of *māyā* as the material cause of creation, we must also question the understanding of liberation that follows from these interpretations. What does it mean to contend that only the knowledge of *nirguṇa-brahman* is liberating knowledge? *Nirguṇa-brahman,* as conceived by these intepreters, is *brahman* without qualities and relations and *brahman* "which is neither the cause nor the creator nor the sustainer nor the destroyer of the universe."[41] This study has argued for an understanding of the terminology of *nirguṇa* and *saguṇa* that is different from the heirarchical and supersessionist viewpoint.[42] There are no distinctions in the nature of *brahman* before or after creation and the language of *nirguṇa* and *saguṇa* are complementary and necessary rather than exclusive.[43] These terms point to *brahman* as both immanent and transcendent, as involved in the world-process and yet free from its limits and as beyond all definitions. In this view, one does not have to deny creatorship to *brahman* or to bifurcate *brahman* in order to preserve *brahman's* non-duality and transcendence.

When *nirguṇa,* on the contrary, is understood as the denial of *brahman* as the cause and creator of the world and when it is argued that only the knowledge of *brahman* as *nirguṇa* is liberative, many problems arise. If *brahman* as the cause of the world is denied, does this not mean that the world is also denied? If the cause is nonexistent, then the effect is also nonexistent. If liberation means the nonexistence of the world, what does this mean for the possibility of living-liberation (*jīvanmukti*)? How does the living-free person encounter and experience the world? The descriptions of the liberated person that are available in the authoritative texts, such as in Bhagavadgītā (2:55–72), reveal a person who is aware of the world, but who is free from greed, fear, and anger in her relationships. She moves about in the world with a freedom that results from self-control and mastering likes and dislikes. It is also important to remember that the knowledge of *brahman,* in the understanding of Śaṅkara, does not result in the obliteration of the world.[44] The world, according to Śaṅkara, "is indeed a fact for those who do not believe in things as different from *brahman* as well as for those who do believe. But the believers of the highest truth, while discussing in accordance with the *śrutis* the actual existence or nonexistence of things apart from *brahman,* conclude that *brahman* alone is the one without a second, beyond all finite relations."[45]

The difference between bondage and liberation is not the existence or nonexistence of the world, since the world is an experienced reality for the liberated and the bound. The difference is that the unliberated person attributes a separate reality to the world, while the liberated sees the world as owing its existence and being to *brahman.* While experiencing the plurality of the world, the liberated knows the truth of its ontological non-duality. There is no need in Advaita to deny creatorship to *brahman* and to deny the world as *brahman's* creation. Such a need arises only from the erroneous view that creatorship and creation compromise the non-dual nature of *brahman.* This, in fact, is a view that Advaita argues against. Creation does not imply transformation in the nature of *brahman,* and the world, in its essential nature, is non-different from *brahman.* The splendor of *brahman* is that it is the source of the many while always being non-dual and limitless.

It is important to remind ourselves that the knowledge that liberates in Advaita is the knowledge of the self's non-duality and its non-difference from *brahman.* As *brahman,* the self is awareness that is unlimited by time and space. The denial of *brahman* as creator and of the world as creation are neither necessary nor required for liberation. The argument made by some commentators that Advaita liberation requires one "to go beyond Īśvara" is not justified. On the contrary, it would be entirely consistent with the Advaita understanding of liberation for the liberated who is experiencing the world to understand it as *brahman*'s creation, while, at the same time, affirming *brahman's* non-duality and the self's identity with *brahman.* The world is seen to be related to *brahman* as effect is related to cause, although, since *brahman* is both material and efficient cause of the world, the world has no separate ontological existence from *brahman.*

On the personal level, it would also be consistent with the Advaita understanding of liberation to know *brahman* as God while also owning *brahman* to be the self. These are not mutually exclusive. Since the world continues to exist after liberation, the *jīvanmukta* who experiences the world accounts for the world and her own existence in it by tracing its origin to *brahman.* She knows *brahman* as the source and sustenance of the world. At the same time, she knows the world and the self to be of the nature of *brahman.* The liberated ones, in Advaita, do not usurp, from *brahman,* the powers of creation and preservation of the universe. These are always exclusive to *brahman.* This is the point argued by Śaṅkara in his commentary on *Brahmasūtra* 4.4.17, where he is responding to the claim that the power of the liberated is unlimited. Śaṅkara's view is that while the liberated may acquire certain powers through God, these never include the power of creation.

> For the supreme Lord alone has competence for activities concerning (the creation etc. of) the universe, inasmuch as the fact of creation etc. is taught in connection with Him alone, and the word "eternal" is attributed to Him. The Upaniṣads mention that others get the divine powers of becoming atomic in size etc. as a result of search and hankering for knowing Him. Thus they are remotely placed from the activities connected with creation etc. of the universe. Moreover, from the very fact that the liberated souls are equipped with minds, they cannot have any unanimity, so that someone may at one time want the continuance of the universe and someone else its destruction; in this way they may at times be opposed to one another. If one should seek a reconciliation by making all other wills dependent on one will only, then that reconciler will perforce arrive at the conclusion that all other wills are dependent on God's will alone.[46]

Liberation is not "going beyond" *brahman* as creator (*īśvara*), but knowing *brahman* as both creator and self. To know *brahman* only as creator enables one to account for the world, but leaves open the possibility of a dualism that radically separates the world from *brahman* and leaves the non-dual nature of *brahman* open to question. Such an understanding, from the Advaita standpoint, is not liberative, since it does not explain the nature of the self in relation to *brahman.* To know *brahman* as the self is liberating, but this alone does not account for the world and its nature in relation to *brahman.* To understand *brahman* as creator and self is a more complex but undoubtedly richer view which liberates, since the self as *brahman* is free, but also enables the liberated one to explain, value, and embrace the world as being of the nature of *brahman.*

Advaita commentators who understand liberative knowledge to mean "going-beyond" *brahman* as God find it difficult to explain Śaṅkara's devotional writings and proffer the rather questionable argument that these compositions were meant for inferior aspirants.[47] "For the benefit of ordinary mortals," claims one writer, "a great Advaitin like Sri Śaṅkara breaks forth into devotional lyrics of ecstatic content in praise of the several aspects of the *saguṇa brahman* in the course of his pilgrimages to the holy shrines in India."[48] It is the a priori argument that Śaṅkara's understanding of *brahman* precludes a devotional relationship which results in such spurious arguments. The deep devotional fervor of these hymns make the argument that they do not express the personal passion of Śaṅkara but were meant for inferior aspirations an unconvincing one.

If one persists with the argument about the questionable authorship of the hymns, we respond by pointing out that many of the authentic works of Śaṅkara begin with invocations to *brahman* as *ātman* and God. The metrical section of *Upadeśasāhasrī* begins with the following verse:

> Salutation to the all-knowing Pure Consciousness which pervades all, is all, abides in the hearts of all beings, and is beyond all objects [of knowledge].

Śaṅkara begins his commentary on the Taittirīya Upaniṣad with an explict salutation to *brahman* as consciousness (*jnānātmane*) and as creator.

> Salutation to that (*brahman*) which is of the nature or consciousness, from which this whole universe was born, into which it gets dissolved, and by which it is sustained.[49]

Many of the Upaniṣads themselves commence their discussions with invocatory verses. One of the most famous of these occurs at the beginning of the Kena Upaniṣad, where *brahman* is invoked for protection and nourishment.[50] This is followed by another verse of invocation in which the non-difference of *brahman* and the universe is acknowledged and in which the wish is expresssed that one be not spurned by *brahman* (*mā mā brahma nirākarot*). All of these suggest that the understanding of *brahman* as self did not preclude the relationship with *brahman* as God and creator.

To know *brahman,* both as God and self, is also consistent with traditional Advaita interpretations of the great sentence (*mahavākya*) from the Chāndogya Upaniṣad (6:8), *tat tvam asi* (That Thou Art). This statement is repeated nine times during a dialogue between the teacher Uddālaka and his son Śvetaketu, and it is central to the Advaita claim for the identity of *ātman* and *brahman.* The subtlety of the Advaita interpretation of *tat tvam asi* is often missed and it can be easily misconstrued as positing an unconditional identity between the human being and God.

In their primary or literal meanings, "That" and "Thou" cannot be identical. At this level of meaning, "Thou" refers to the finite individual human being, the egocentric psychophysical entity who, according to Śaṅkara, is the hearer, thinker, and the inquirer. As an aggregate of body, sense organs, and mind the individual (*jīva*) is limited in knowledge and capacity. The primary meaning of "That" is *brahman,* the omniscient and omnipotent source of the world. It would be absurd to posit identity between a limited egotistic individual and the unlimited *brahman.* The characteristics of both are contradictory. The human being, however, is not merely a composite of the body, senses, and mind. In the Advaita tradition, these are essentially inert and enlivened only by the presence of *brahman* as awareness. As awareness, *brahman* is the being of the finite individual, the ontological ground and source of the ego or the "I" thought. The ego (*aham vṛtti* or *ahaṁkara*) has no existence or reality apart from *brahman.* As in the example of clay and a clay jar, *brahman* constitutes the essential nature of the ego, although the reverse of this statement is not true. The characteristics of the ego, such as limited knowledge and power, do not belong to *brahman.*

The identity that is posited in *tat tvam asi,* therefore, is not between the limited, egocentric individual and the limitless *brahman.* It identifies, for the benefit of Śvetaketu, that *brahman* is his own self and that, in his essential nature, he in non-different from *brahman.* He is non-different in essential nature from *brahman* just as all things, in their essential nature, are non-different from *brahman.* Śvetaketu does not constitute the nature of *brahman; brahman* constitutes the nature of Śvetaketu.

This teaching about his nature is meant for Śvetaketu as individual being and not for *brahman* who, as awareness, is the source of the ego's consciousness and which, in the analogy of Śaṅkara, has entered Śvetaketu as the sun enters into water and other reflecting surfaces, endowing Śvetaketu with life and luminosity. Although *brahman* constitutes the nature of the ego, the latter, owing to ignorance, does not own its nature as *brahman,* but identifies itself with its psychophysical aggregate and becomes subject to sorrow and suffering. Understanding, through the meaning of a statement such as *tat tvam asi,* that it is *brahman* which constitutes its ground and being and not the instruments of body and mind, is liberative because it frees us from mortality and other ignorance-born sources of anxiety and fear.

Understanding that in its true nature it is not different from *brahman* does not lead to an obliteration of the ego or I-thought. It retains its characteristics as cognizer and thinker. Śaṅkara does not suggest anywhere the absence of a mind in liberation. What is eliminated is ignorance about its essential nature. The knowledge that *brahman* constitutes its essential nature does not also negate all differences between the individual (*jīva*) and *brahman.* The individual still acknowledges *brahman* as the source of the world and the dependence of the world, of which she is a part, on *brahman* for its existence, while also understanding herself to be ontologically non-different from *brahman.* The nuanced understanding of *tat tvam asi,* at the implied rather than literal level, makes this possible. The knowledge of *brahman* as the *ātman* does not confer upon the individual the omnipotence or omniscience of *brahman.*

Notes

INTRODUCTION

1. Eliot Deutsch, *Advaita Vedānta: A Philosophical Reconstruction* (Honolulu: University of Hawaii Press, 1985), 3.

2. For an excellent summary of contemporary scholarship on the dating of Śaṅkara and issues of authorship see, Bradley J. Malkovsky, *The Role of Divine Grace in the Soteriology of Śaṅkarācārya* (Leiden: Brill, 2001), 1–33.

3. Anantanand Rambachan, *Accomplishing the Accomplished: The Vedas as a Source of Valid Knowledge in Śaṅkara* (Honolulu: University of Hawaii Press, 1991).

4. Anantanand Rambachan, *The Limits of Scripture: Vivekananda's Reinterpretation of the Vedas* (Honolulu: University of Hawaii Press, 1994).

5. The works of Paul Hacker and Sengaku Mayeda, among others, are important contributions to these tasks.

6. For Śaṅkara's refutation of the Jain viewpoint see BSBh 2.2.33.

7. The word *experience*, in relation to the *ātman*, is problematic since it suggests duality and objectifies the self. This is a matter to which we return later.

CHAPTER 1. THE HUMAN PROBLEM

1. See CU ch.7. The Upaniṣads are religio/philosophical dialogues between teachers and students found at the end of the authoritative Hindu scriptures, the Vedas. For this reason, the dialogues are called Vedānta (the end of the Vedas). The Vedas are arranged in four collections known as the Ṛgveda, Sāmaveda, Yajurveda, and Atharvaveda. To emphasize the fact that the Vedas were transmitted orally from teacher to student, the texts are collectively referred to as *śruti* (that which is heard). Upaniṣad translations, except where stated otherwise, are taken from *Upaniṣads,* trans. Patrick Olivelle (Oxford: Oxford University Press, 1996).

2. See BU ch.4.

3. The four stages (*āśramas*) are studenthood (*brahmacarya*), householder (*gṛhastya*), forestdweller (*vānaprasthya*), and renunciation (*sannyāsa*).

4. See MU ch.1 Although the terms *parā* and *aparā* are usually translated as "higher" and "lower," it is accurate to understand these as signifying "complete" and "incomplete." The Muṇḍaka Upaniṣad begins with the question from Śaunaka, "What is it, my lord, by knowing which a man comes to know the whole world?" The Upaniṣad suggests that by knowing *brahman,* the cause of everything, one comes to know, in essence, the world. In this sense, the knowledge of *brahman* is *parā* (complete).

5. The attitude and outlook that engender maturity in a student and that qualify her for inquiry into the scriptures will be discussed in ch.2 It is also possible that the Upaniṣad has in mind the first sections of each Veda dealing with ritual action.

6. *parā yathā tadaksharamadhigamyate.*

7. MU 1.1.6.

8. *bhajagovindaṁ bhajagovindaṁ*
bhajagovindaṁ mūḍhamate
saṁprāpte sannihite kāle
na hi na hi rakṣati ḍūkṛñkaraṇe

See T. M. P. Mahadevan, *The Hymns of Śaṅkara* (Delhi: Motilal Banarsidass, 1980). The *Bhajagovindam* is not considered to be an authentic work of Śaṇkara.

9. The reference to the Hindu tradition is not meant to equate Hinduism with Advaita. What is spoken of today as Hinduism is a family of traditions, sharing common features and maintaining distinctive orientations.

10. *nahi daridra sama dukha jaga māhīṁ.* See *Śrī Rāmacaritamānasa,* trans. R. C. Prasad (Delhi: Motilal Banarsidass, 1991), Uttarakāṅḍa, 784.

11. Ibid., Uttarakāṇḍa, 705.

12. BG 3:12. Translations, except where stated otherwise, are taken from *The Bhagavad Gītā,* trans. Winthrop Sargeant (Albany: State University of New York Press, 1984).

13. In BU 5.2.1–3, *dāna* (generosity), *dama* (self-control), and *dayā* (compassion) are listed as cardinal virtues.

14. See BG 3:36–37; 5:23.

15. BG 16: 13–14. For complete profile see 16: 8–18.

16. Huston Smith, *The World's Religions* (New York: HarperCollins, 1991), 15.

17. KaU 1:18.

18. KaU 1: 26–27.

19. David Loy, "The Religion of the Market," *Journal of the American Academy of Religion* 65, no. 2 (1997): 286.

20. *dharmāviruddha bhūteṣu kāmo 'smi bharatarṣabha.* My translation.

21. BG 5:22

22. Quoted in William James, *The Varieties of Religious Experience* (Glasgow: William Collins, 1979), 160.

23. *parīkṣya lokān karmacitān brāhmaṇo*
nirvedamāyānnāstyakṛtaḥ kṛtena
tadvijñānārtham sa gurumevābhigacchet
samitpāṇiḥ śrotriyaṁ brahmaniṣṭham

My translation. The text specifically addresses a *brahmin* (a member of the highest caste) since the upper castes were the ones traditionally entitled to the study of the scriptures.

24. The word *brahman* is derived from the Sanskrit root *bṛh*—"to grow" or "to expand." It is used in the Upaniṣads to refer to the absolute reality that is the source and ground of all that exists. In the TU (3.1) *brahman* is described as that from which all beings are born, that by which they live, and that into which they return.

25. CU 7.1.3.
śrutam hy eva me bhagavad-dṛśebhyaḥ tarati śokam ātmavid iti so'ham bhagavaḥ, śocāmi, tam mā bhagavān, sokasya pāram tārayatv iti

CHAPTER 2. THE REQUIREMENTS OF DISCIPLESHIP

1. *tasmai sa vidvānupasannāya samyak*
praśāntacittāya śamānvitāya
yenākṣaraṁ puruṣaṁ veda satyaṁ
provāca tāṁ tatvato brahmavidyām. My translation.

2. *nāvirato duścaritan nāśānto nāsamāhitaḥ*
nāśānta mānaso vāpi prajñānenainam āpnuyāt (KaU 2.24). My translation.

3. *satyena labhyas tapasā hy eṣa ātmā samyaj-jñānena brahmacaryeṇa nityam*
antaḥ-śarīre jyotir-mayo hi śubro yam paśyanti yatayaḥ kṣīṇdoṣaḥ (MU 3.1.5).

For a longer list see BG 13:8–12.

4. This is not to deny that knowing the nature of anger in one's own mind may help in understanding its expression in another.

5. *brahma veda brahmaiva bhavati.* My translation.

6. Sara Grant, *Toward An Alternative Theology* (Notre Dame: University of Notre Dame Press, 2002), 54–55.

7. *sarvabhūtastham ātmānam sarvabhūtani ca 'tmani.*

8. BG 6:32. Also 5:25 and 12:4.

9. KeUBh 4.8, 93–94. Also ŚvU 6:21–23.

10. BGBh 6:26, 197.

11. BSBh I.1.1, 9. The *Brahmasūtra*, also referred to as the *Vedāntasūtra*, is attributed to Bādarāyaṇa (c.400 BCE). In this work, the author attempts a systematic exposition of the Upaniṣads in the *sūtra* style of short, condensed statements. It is divided into four sections. The first section is concerned with establishing that *brahman* is the subject matter of the Upaniṣads, the second section deals with objections by various rival schools, the third section discusses the means for the attainment of *brahman*, and the fourth considers the results of the knowledge of *brahman*. The *Brahmasūtra*, together with the Upaniṣads and the Bhagavadgītā, are considered to be the triple foundation (*prasthāna-traya*) of the Advaita tradition.

12. For the purpose of defining these values, I have drawn from various Vedānta treatises including the writings of Śaṅkara, the *Vedāntasāra* of Sadananda (c. 15th century), the *Vedāntaparibhāṣa* of Dharmarāja Adhvarīndra (c. 17th century), and the

Tattvabodha, a text of Advaita definitions. This is a work of unknown authorship and wrongly attributed to Śaṇkara. There is general agreement about these definitions within the tradition. See also US II. I. 2.

13. See, for example, KaU 3:12.

14. Cited in Bradley J. Malkovsky, *The Role of Divine Grace in the Soteriology of Śaṅkarācārya*, 80.

15. *Bhajagovindam* Vs.16.

16. BG 2:59.

17. BG 3:6.

18. BG 2:32; 2:37.

19. *te taṁ bhuktvā svargalokaṁ viśālam kśīṇe puṇye martyalokaṁ viśanti.*

20. *Uparama* is defined differently in various Advaita treatises. The *Vedānta Paribhāṣa,* for example, defines it as the absence of distractions (*vikṣepābhāva*). In this sense, it may be understood as a consequence of the achievement of *śama* and *dama. Tattva Bodha* presents it as fulfillment of obligatory duty (*svadharmānuṣṭānameva*). I have chosen to follow the latter interpretation.

21. See, for example, BG 18:41–44.

22. Such an understanding of the meaning of *uparama* may bring it closer to Buddhist ideas of right livelihood. In some Advaita accounts, *uparama* is equated with renunciation. This is an alternative understanding offered in the *Vedāntasāra.*

23. In the *Vivekacūḍāmaṇi,* a philosophical poem wrongly attributed to Śaṅkara, the author defines *titikṣa* as, "the bearing of all afflictions without caring to redress them, being free (at the same time) from anxiety or lament on their score." See *Vivekacūḍāmaṇi,* trans. Swami Madhavananda (Calcutta: Advaita Ashrama, 1978), Vs.24.

24. This seems to be the unanimous interpretation of the commentators (*guruvedāntavākyeṣu viśvāsaḥ*).

25. Svarupa Chaitanya, for example, writes of *śraddhā* as "unqualified faith in the teacher and the scriptures. . . . The teacher and the scriptures always say the same thing but sometimes the teacher amplifies or supplements the scriptural statements to suit the level of the student." See Svarupa Chaitanya, *Tattva Bodha of Sankaracharya* (Bombay: Central Chinmaya Mission Trust, 1993).

26. See, for example, KaU 3:12.

27. *Vedāntasāra* 1.30.

28. *sa ho ya vai tat paramam brahma veda brahmaiva bhavati*
tarati śokaṁ tarati pāpmānaṁ guhā-granthibhyo vimukto'-mṛto bhavati.

29. *mṛtyu-proktāṁ naciketo' tha labdhva vidyām etām yogavidhim ca kṛtsnam*
brahmaprāpto virajo 'bhūd vimṛtyur anyopy evam yo vid
adhyātmam eva.

30. Swami Dayananda Saraswati, *Introduction to Vedānta* (Delhi: Vision Books, 1989), 110.

31. *vedānte paramaṁ guhyam purākalpe pracoditam*
nāpraśāntāya dātavyam nāputrāyāśiṣyāya va punaḥ

yasya deve parā bhaktir yathā deve tathā gurau
tasyaite kathitā hy arthāḥ prakāśante mahātmanaḥ prakāśante mahātmanaḥ.

My translation.

32. *kriyāvantas śrotriya brahmaniṣṭhās svayaṁ juhvata ekarṣim śraddhayantaḥ*
teṣām evaitām brahma-vidyāṁ vadeta śirovrataṁ vidhivad yais tu cīrṇam.

See also BG 18:67.

33. See BSBh 1.3.34, 230.

34. BSBh 1.3.38, 233–234.

35. See Michael Comans, *The Method of Early Vedānta* (Delhi: Motilal Banarsidass, 2000), 317. In spite of his explanation, Comans is not untroubled and concedes that "if Śaṅkara had wished to argue the opposite, radical view, that Śūdras ought to be entitled to Vedic study, it would not have been impossible for someone of his ability to mount a substantial argument in favour of that position . . ." We must wrestle still with the reason why he did not do so.

36. See, for example, G. C. Pande, *Life and Thought of Śaṅkarācārya* (Delhi: Motilal Banarsidass, 1994), 249–250. We cannot explain away Śaṅkara's endorsement of caste eligibility by contending, as Pande does, "that in commenting on the classical texts Śaṅkara is necessarily bound by their plain views and the *Smṛtis* by his time clearly expressed discriminatory views as far as the rights of the Śūdras to Vedic study and ritual were concerned." The creative intellect of Śaṅkara need not be so constrained if his convictions differed.

CHAPTER 3. THE NATURE OF THE *ĀTMAN*

1. *The Varieties of Religious Experience,* 147.

2. *kasminnu bhagavo vijñāte sarvamidaṁ vijñātaṁ bhavatīti.* My translation.

3. See also the questions at the commencement of the discussion in Kena and Praśna Upaniṣads. Kena begins with an inquiry about the source of life in the body, while the student in Praśna wants to know about the origin of life itself.

4. CU 7.24.1.

5. My translation.

6. See BUBh 1.4.7, 83; TUBh 2.1.1, 300. I have expanded the translator's summary.

7. BUBh 2.1.20, 210.

8. See CUBh 6.14.2, 352–53.

9. See Arthur Osborne, *Ramana Maharshi and the Path of Self-Knowledge* (New York: Samuel Weiser, 1970), 83.

10. BSBh introduction, 1. There are also references to this method throughout US.

11. "It is the innate assumption of people that the *Ātman* is not distinct from the body and the like. This arises from nescience." US I.1.16.

12. See Swami Dayananda Saraswati, *The Teaching of the Bhagavadgītā* (Rishikesh: Sri Gangadhareswar Trust, 1985), 31. The point here is whether the body is an object of knowledge or not.

13. "Just as oneself is not the body which is seen wandering about begging alms in the dreaming state, so he is different from the body which is seen in the waking state, since he is the seer [of the body]." US I.14.2.

14. "So also one superimposes the attributes of the senses and organs when one thinks, "I am dumb," "I have lost one eye," "I am a eunuch," "I am deaf," or "I am blind." BSBh 1.1.1, 6.

15. The mind, because of its subtlety, is not considered to be available for perception, internal or external. Its expression in thoughts and emotions, however, is known to the self.

16. Swami Dayananda Saraswati, *The Teaching of the Bhagavadgītā,* 34.

17. Swami Nikhilananda, trans., *Dṛg Dṛśya Viveka* (Mysore: Sri Ramakrishna Ashrama, 1970). While traditionally attributed to Śaṅkara, this work (also known as *Vākyasudhā*) is not regarded by most scholars as authentic. Nikhilananda attributes it to Bhāratītīrtha (c. fourteenth century).

18. Translation modified.

19. This analysis is traditionally referred to as *pañcakośa prakriyā*. The term, *kośa* (sheath) is not used in the Taittīriya Upaniṣad 2.5, where this discussion occurs.

20. See *Vedāntasāra,* ch.2, and *Vedāntaparibhāṣa,* ch.7. Advaita describes a complex process called *pañcīkaraṇa*, or quintuplication, whereby the five subtle elements out of which the subtle body is formed undergo a process of evolution and combination with each other to form the compounded or gross elements.

21. See BGBh 2:20, 41–42.

22. Translation modified.

23. See BG 2:24.

24. See BG 2:22.

25. John Grimes, *Problems and Perspectives in Religious Discourse: Advaita Vedānta Implications* (Albany: State University of New York Press, 1994), 82.

26. See also CU 7.23.1 and TU 2.7, and 3.6.

27. For an insightful treatment of Śaṅkara's discussion of *brahman* as *ānanda*, see Andrew O. Fort, "Beyond Pleasure: Śaṅkara on Bliss," *Journal of Indian Philosophy* 16, no.2 (1988): 177–89.

28. See chapter 6.

29. For a detailed treatment of Śaṅkara's exegesis of Taittirīya Upaniṣad 2.1.1., see Anantanand Rambachan, *Accomplishing the Accomplished,* 72–76.

30. BUBh 3.9.28.7, 396.

31. See *Vedāntaparibhāṣa*, ch.8.

32. TUBh 2.8.1–4, 367.

33. TUBh 2.8.1–4, 367–68. See also 2.5.1, 338.

34. TUBh 2.7.1, 359–60.

35. Swami Dayananda Saraswati, *The Teaching of the Bhagavadgītā,* 34–35.

36. Peter Russell, *From Science to God* (Novato: New World Library, 2003), 83–84.

37. This complex subject is treated in detail in chapter 5, but it is necessary to state the central thesis here since this chapter focuses primarily on distinguishing the *ātman* as awareness.

CHAPTER 4. THE SOURCE OF VALID KNOWLEDGE

1. I have discussed this question in several publications. My most detailed treatment will be found in *Accomplishing the Accomplished: The Vedas as a Source of Valid Knowledge in Śaṅkara.*

2. *Vedāntaparibhāṣa,* ch.1.

3. See BSBh 1.1.4, 34.

4. BUBh 2.1.20, 214.

5. BUBh 4.3.6, 425. Advaita accepts six sources of valid knowledge. These are: perception (*pratyakṣa*), inference (*anumāna*), comparison (*upamāna*), postulation (*arthāpatti*), non-cognition (*anupalabdhi*), and the Vedas (*śabda*). For a brief discussion of the nature and function of each type see, *Accomplishing the Accomplished,* 23–29. Śaṅkara does not undertake any systematic analysis of the sources of valid knowledge. He appears to treat these as well known. In a listing in BUBh 3.3.1, 312, he omits non-cognition.

6. BSBh 2.1.6, 313.

7. BSBh 2.1.11, 322. Also KaUBh 1.2.8–9, 138–141. While rejecting independent reasoning as a means of knowledge for *brahman,* Śaṅkara is supportive of arguments which depend upon the revelations of the Vedas. Halbfass correctly captured Śaṅkara's position in his description that reason "has its legitimate role under the guidance of and in cooperation with *śruti.*" See Wilhelm Halbfass, *Tradition and Reflection: Explorations in Indian Thought* (Albany: State University of New York Press, 1991), 154.

8. See BUBh introduction, 2–3.

9. The *sūtras* of Jaimini (ca. 200 BCE) are the earliest systematic work of this school. Jaimini's work consists of 2,644 *sūtras.* See Ganganatha Jha, trans., *The Pūrva Mīmāṁsā Sūtras of Jaimini* (Varanasi: Bharatiya Publishing House, 1979).

10. For Śaṅkara, the word *upaniṣad* refers primarily to the knowledge of *brahman* and only secondarily to texts. See BUBh 1.1, 1.

11. The position that the *śruti* only affords indirect or mediate knowledge enjoys wide popularity and continues to be expounded. In a recent work on the Upaniṣads, for example, R. Puligandla contends that following mediate knowledge from the texts, the student "undertakes *dhyana* (Yogic meditation) on the central *advaitic* truth of the non-difference of *Brahman* (ultimate non-dual reality) and *Atman* (one's true being, pure consciousness). Through prolonged and intense meditation, he comes to see in a flash of non-dual intuition—*prajna*—that he is indeed *Brahman,* the sole reality." See R. Puligandla, *That Thou Art: Wisdom of the Upanishads* (California: Asian Humanities Press, 2002), 105.

12. BSBh 1.1.1, 11.

13. BSBh 2.3.7, 455.

14. BSBh 1.1.4, 36–37.

15. BSBh 1.1.4, 26–36.

16. TUBh 1.11.4, 284.

17. TUBh 1.11.4, 287.

18. BUBh 1.4.7, 96.

19. We must remember that since bliss is the nature of *brahman,* the word *experience* may be misleading and suggestive of dualism. *Ānanda* as indicative of the nature of *brahman* is non-dual.

20. The character of the liberated person is treated in more detail in ch.7.

21. BUBh 1.4.7, 92.

22. The word *experience* in relation to the self is problematic, since it suggests encountering something as an object. Awareness, being the nature of the self, is never experienced as an object.

23. BUBh 4.4.20, 518.

24. See Rambachan, *Accomplishing the Accomplished,* 44–46.

25. The Upaniṣads are referred to as *Vedānta vākyas* (*Vedānta* sentences), because they occur at the end (*anta*) of the Vedas and are believed to embody the highest wisdom of these texts.

26. BGBh 2:21, 46.

27. BSBh 1.1.2, 16–17.

28. Śaṅkara, unlike later Advaitins, does not appear particularly interested in any analytical treatment of *avidyā.* His approach is more pragmatic and concerned with establishing the nature of *brahman* and the overcoming of ignorance. See Paul Hacker, "Distinctive Features of the Doctrine and Terminology of Śaṅkara: Avidyā, Nāmarūpa, Māyā, Īśvara" in *Philology and Confrontation,* ed. Wilhelm Halbfass (Albany: State University of New York Press, 1995), 58–67. Hereafter abbreviated "Distinctive Features." For a good example of Śaṅkara's pragmatic approach, see BGBh 13:2, 332–33.

29. BSBh 1.1.1, 6.

30. Like all good analogies, this one also has its limits. The self is not spatially separate from anything and thus a reflection is not possible. This analogy is still widely used. See Carol Whitfield, "The Jungian Myth and Advaita Vedanta" (Unpublished PhD dissertation, Graduate Theological Union, 1992).

31. MUBh 2.1.8, 155–156.

32. BGBh 13:11, 343.

33. BGBh 18:50, 487–488.

34. See also BUBh 4.4.19, 517.

35. I am not concerned, in this discussion, with the question of how the words of the scripture, finite and conventional in nature, can teach about the infinite *brahman.* For finite words to be used to indicate the infinite, they must be wielded and used skillfully. This is the task of the teacher, and I have discussed some of the traditional methods in an earlier publication. See *Accomplishing the Accomplished,* ch.3. See also Michael Comans, *The Method of Early Advaita Vedānta,* 284–300.

36. See US 1. 17, 61–80.

37. KeUBh 1.4, 51.

38. BUBh 4.4.6, 503–504.

39. MUBh 3.1.8, 156.

40. I believe that the dilemma of knowing the knower, discussed in this chapter, has led many commentators to suggest that the knowledge of *brahman* is gained through a special mind-transcending experience equated with the *nirvikalpa samādhi* of Yoga. This point of view has been questioned and refuted by Michael Comans in an excellent discussion, "The Question of the Importance of *Samādhi* in Modern and Classical Advaita Vedānta," in *Philosophy East and West,* 43, no.1 (1993): 19–38. Śaṅkara, argues Comans, makes sparing use of the word *samādhi* and does not set up the attainment of *nirvikalpa samādhi* as a goal. The contemplation recommended by Śaṅkara is one that aims at the discernment of the ever-present self. See also Michael Comans, "Śaṅkara and the Prasaṅkhyānavada," in *Journal of Indian Philosophy,* 24 (1996): 49–71. The author refutes interpretations of Śaṅkara suggesting that the Upaniṣads are incapable of directly engendering liberating knowledge.

41. BSBh 2.1.10, 319.

42. See, for example, CU 6.14.1–2, 351–53.

43. For a discussion of the teacher see, Swami Dayananda Saraswati, *Introduction to Vedānta.*

44. MUBh 1.2.13, 111.

45. BSBh 1.1.3, 19.

46. See TUBh 2.9.1, 385–88, for Śaṅkara's commentary on this significant text.

47. "That from which these beings are born; on which, once born, they live; and into which they pass upon death—seek to know that! That is *brahman,*" TU 3.1.1. Translation modified.

48. See CU 6.1.4–6.

49. See BGBh 13:12, 345.

50. See KeUBh 2.1, 62–63.

51. BUBh 1.4.7, 95. In his commentary on BU 2.3.6, 39, Śaṅkara includes the term *brahman,* along with *ātman,* as not definitive of the essential nature of *brahman.*

52. KeU 2.3. Gambhirananda's translation.

53. BG 2:29.

CHAPTER 5. *BRAHMAN* AS THE WORLD

1. Malkovsky has correctly argued that the term *advaita* does not seek so much to define *brahman,* but to correct a false understanding of reality. It is only indirectly a statement about *brahman.* See Bradley Malkovsky, "Advaita Vedanta and Christian Faith," *Journal of Ecumenical Studies* 36 no. 3–4 (Summer-Fall 1999): 397–422.

2. See, for example, R. Balasubramanian, "The Absolute and God," in *The Tradition of Advaita,* ed. R. Balasubramanian (Delhi: Munshiram Manoharlal, 1994), 28–30.

3. Eliot Deutsch, *Advaita Vedānta: A Philosophical Reconstruction,* 28.

4. T. M. P. Mahadevan, *Outlines of Hinduism* (Bombay: Chetana Limited, 1977), 147.

5. Swami Nirvedananda, *Hinduism at a Glance* (Calcutta: Ramakrishna Mission, 1979), 172.

6. See S. Dasgupta, *A History of Indian Philosophy* (Delhi: Motilal Banarsidass, 1975), I:442. This is the most widely advocated interpretation of Śaṅkara. For similar views see P. Deussen, *System of the Vedānta* (Delhi: Oriental Reprint, 1979), 459; M. Hiriyanna, *Essentials of Indian Philosophy* (London: Unwin Paperbacks, 1978), 158; and Swami Prabhavananda, *The Spiritual Heritage of India* (Hollywood: Vedanta Press, 1979), 284. Prabhavananda contends that, with knowledge of *brahman,* the world is not experienced and ceases to exist.

7. *The Tales and Parables of Sri Ramakrishna* (Madras: Sri Ramakrishna Math, 1980), 52–54.

8. It will be obvious that in many of these passages, the Upaniṣads use the words *ātman* and *brahman* interchangeably, emphasizing their identity.

9. While I have cited some of the creation texts, I need to emphasize that, for the Advaita tradition, the purpose of the Upaniṣads is not to reveal the order of the creation. The central purpose of revelation is the identity of the self and *brahman.* Admitting that there are apparent conflicts in Upaniṣadic texts describing the sequence of creation, Śaṅkara, in an important comment (BSBh 1.4.14, 265), explains that " it cannot be said that the conflict of statements concerning the world affects the statements concerning the cause, i.e. Brahman, in which all the Vedānta-texts are seen to agree—for that would be an altogether unfounded generalization;—and, in the second place, the teacher will reconcile later on (II,3) those conflicting passages also which refer to the world. And, to consider the matter more thoroughly, a conflict of statements regarding the world would not even matter greatly, since the creation of the world and similar topics are not at all what Scripture wishes to teach." Thibaut trans. Such topics, for Śaṅkara, do not have direct benefits and are secondary to the revelation of *brahman.*

10. While translating *upādāna kāraṇa* as "material cause," there is no suggestion that *brahman* is material. R. De Smet speaks wisely of *upādāna kāraṇa* in relation to *brahman* as "reality-providing" cause to emphasize that there is no transformation in the nature of *brahman.* See Malkovsky, *The Role of Divine Grace,* 62.

11. *ayam atmā brahma*

12. *pūrṇamadaḥ pūrṇamidaṁ pūrṇāt pūrṇamudacyate*
pūrṇasya pūrṇamādāya pūrṇamevāvaśiṣyate

13. My summary.

14. To speak of *brahman* becoming the many will be problematic if it suggests an actual transformation in nature.

15. For elaborations of this understaning of *māyā* and its relationship to *brahman,* see, for example, P. Sankaranarayanan, *What Is Advaita?* (Bombay: Bharatiya Vidya Bhavan, 1988), ch.5 and Y.Keshava Menon, *The Mind of Shankara* (Bombay: Jaico Publishing House, 1976), 50–65. R. Balasubramanian describes *māyā* as the transformative material cause of the physical universe. See R. Balasubramanian, "Advaita: An Overview," in *The Tradition of Advaita,* 18–19.

16. See Srinivasa Rao, "Two Myths in Advaita," *Journal of Indian Philosophy* 24, no. 3 (June 1996): 265–79.

17. Paul Hacker has already called attention to Śaṅkara's infrequent use of *māyā*, compared to *nāmārūpa* and *avidyā*. *Māyā* becomes a matter of greater concern to later exponents of Advaita. Hacker points out that Śaṅkara never refers to the tradition as *māyāvāda*. He concludes that "*māyā*, for Śaṅkara, is not the cause or the substance of what is illusory, but the illusory is compared with *māyā*, or else it is said that the illusory is *māyā*." See "Distinctive Features," 78–80.

18. BSBh.1.1.2, 14.

19. Ibid. Also 1.1.9, 60; 1.1.10, 60–61; 1.1.11, 61; 2.1.1, 301–302.

20. BSBh 2.1.24, 351.

21. This view is technically referred to as *satkāryavāda*, or the cause-effect non-difference doctrine. It advocates that effects are preexistent in their causes and non-different. An effect manifests what was hitherto latent in its cause. It is not new and different from its cause.

22. Michael Comans, *The Method of Early Vedānta*, concludes that post-Śaṅkara Advaitins "have tended to materialize *avidyā-māyā* and treat it as a virtual reality in its own right." He suggests that this may be the consequence of the influence of the Sāṅkhya doctrine of *prakṛti*. See 263–64.

23. Rao, "Two Myths in Advaita," 267–68.

24. Ibid., 268.

25. BSBh 2.2.44, 442.

26. BSBh 2.1.6, 312.

27. See Jacob Kattackal, *Religion and Ethics in Advaita* (Frieburg: Herder, 1980), 71–72.

28. BSBh 2.1.6, 313.

29. BSBh 2.1.9, 318.

30. BSBh 3.2.21, 620.

31. CUBh 6.1.4–7, 293–95.

32. BSBh 2.1.9, 317–18.

33. Rao, "Two Myths in Advaita," 268. Śaṅkara also makes the same point for ontological dependence in BSBh 2.1.9, 318, when he argues that the "effect is recognized to be equally non-different from the cause during all three periods of time."

34. Advaita, as already indicated, subscribes to the doctrine of *satkāryavada*, which proposes the non-difference of cause and effect. This doctrine has two variations. Those who subscribe to the *pariṇāmavada* version, like Sāṅkhya, hold that the effect is a real transformation of the cause. Advaita subscribes to the *vivartavāda* version, which proposes that the effect does not represent a transformation in the nature of the cause. Change in the nature of the cause is apparent only.

35. BSBh 2.2.28, 420.

36. BSBh 2.2.29, 423–24. Also, 2.2.30, 424–25. Srinivasa Rao also points out that Śaṅkara, in his commentary on the *Brahmasūtra*, never uses the word *mithyā* (illusion) to describe the world. Śaṅkara makes frequent use of the word *mithyā* to characterize

wrong knowledge of *brahman,* but never to define the nature of the world. See Rao, "Two Myths in Advaita," 272–73.

37. The Catholic theologian Richard De Smet affirms a similar understanding between Śaṅkara and Thomas Aquinas. See Bradley Malkovsky, " Advaita Vedānta and Christian Faith," 410–15.

38. These are discussed in most works on Advaita. See, for example, Eliot Deutsch, *Advaita Vedānta: A Philosophical Reconstruction,* ch.2.

39. Ramakrishna Puligandla, *Jñāna-Yoga—The Way of Knowledge* (Lanham: University Press of America, 1985), 87.

40. Eliot Deutsch, *Advaita Vedānta,* 15.

41. BSBh 2.2.29, 423–24.

42. TUBh 2.6.1, 355–56.

43. BSBh 2.1.16, 337.

44. The similarity between this opponent's argument and some contemporary formulations of Advaita is remarkable in the call for the eradication of plurality as a precondition of knowing *brahman.*

45. BSBh 3.2.21, 620.

46. BUBh 3.5.1, 333.

47. D. M. Datta, "Some Realistic Aspects of the Philosophy of Śaṅkara," in *Recent Indian Philosophy,* ed. Kalidas Bhattacharya (Calcutta: Progressive Publishers, 1963), I: 345.

48. BSBh 2.1.9, 318.

49. BSBh 2.1.16, 337.

50. My translation. See also ĪU 1, 6; KaU 2:22; MU 3.2.5.

CHAPTER 6. *BRAHMAN* AS GOD

1. S. R. Bhatt, "Some Reflections on Advaita Vedāntic Concepts of Māyā and Avidyā," in *The Tradition of Advaita,* 112.

2. See, for example, R. Puligandla, *Fundamentals of Indian Philosophy* (Nashville: Abingdon Press, 1975), 225–26. Although *parā* and *aparā* also connote complete and incomplete, most Advaita commentators interpret these as higher and lower. It is this viewpoint that concerns us here.

3. Instructive here is Hacker's conclusion that the sharp distinction between *saguna-nirguṇa brahman* is more characteristic of post-Śaṅkara Advaita. Śaṅkara is more fluid in his terminolgy and uses the terms *īśvara, parameśvara, paramātman,* and *para brahman* to refer to the absolute. See "Distinctive Features," 85–96. Also Comans, *The Method of Early Advaita Vedānta,* 215–25.

4. P. Sankaranarayanan, *What Is Advaita?* 46. For a good summary of this point of view, see Bradley Malkovsky, "The Personhood of Saṁkara's *Para Brahman,*" *The Journal of Religion* 77 (1997): 541–62.

5. *Fundamentals of Indian Philosophy,* 225.

6. R, Balasubramanian, "The Absolute and God," in *The Tradition of Advaita,* 36. P. T. Raju appears to cite, with approval, the view of Radhakrishnan that God is only a thought-product. See P. T. Raju, *The Structural Depths of Indian Thought (*Albany: State University of New York Press, 1985), 395.

7. See Swami Satprakashananda, *The Universe, God and God-Realization* (St. Louis: The Vedanta Society of St. Louis, 1977), 77.

8. R. Puligandla, *That Thou Art: The Wisdom of the Upanishads,* 89.

9. See, for example, AU 1.1.1–2; TU 2.6.1; CU 6.2.3; PU 1.4.

10. Richard De Smet has correctly argued that the relationship between *brahman* and the world is logical and not ontological. Again, he sees this as similar to the position of Thomas Aquinas. See Bradley J. Malkovsky, "The Life and Work of Richard V. De Smet, S. J.," in Bradley J. Malkovsky, ed., *New Perspectives on Advaita Vedanta* (Leiden: Brill, 2000), 14–17.

11. This is an example of the application of the method of *adhyāropa* and *apavāda* to decriptions of *brahman.* See Rambachan, *Accomplishing the Accomplished,* 67–72. I am not aware of the specific application of this method to the issue of action and relation in *brahman.*

12. See, for example, AU 1.1 and CU 6.2.1.

13. It is this understanding of the nature of *brahman* that particularly distinguishes the theology of Advaita from Viśiṣṭādvaita. In the latter, *brahman* enjoys an internal differentiation of matter and selves.

14. BGBh 13.12, 346–47.

15. *yato vāco nivartante aprāpya manasā saha*

16. For a discussion of this distinction, see Karl H. Potter, *Advaita Vedānta up to Śaṅkara and His Pupils* (The Encyclopedia of Indian Philosophies, Vol. III.) (Delhi: Motilal Banarsidass, 1981), 73–76.

17. See TU 2.1.1. Śaṅkara does not regard these words as directly indicating the nature of *brahman.*

18. *āptakāmasya kā spṛhā*

19. *loka vat līlā kaivalyam*

20. Michael Comans, *The Method of Early Advaita Vedānta,* 188.

21. This view may come quite close to an argument for spontaneous creation, a doctrine explicitly rejected by Śaṅkara.

22. BSBh 2.1.33, 361.

23. Swami Gambhirananda's translation. Olivelle translated, "Let me multiply myself. Let me produce offspring." The desire for offspring is also mentioned in PU 1.4.

24. We have already commented critically, in chapter 3, on the translation of *ānanda* as bliss.

25. Gauḍapāda's argument may be construed as a rebuttal of the view that creation is an accidental attribute of *brahman.*

26. G. Lynn Stephens and Gregory Pence, *Seven Dilemmas in World Religions* (New York: Paragon House, 1994), 91. The point of the MU (1.1.7) analogies is not

to suggest the absence of deliberation on the part of *brahman* but the identity of intelligent and material cause and the freedom from dependence on accessories.

27. See also PU 6.3. and 1.4.

28. BSBh 1.4.15, 275.

29. Thibaut's translation, 16–17.

30. For a discussion of some of the uses of this example, see Karl H. Potter, ed., *Encyclopedia of Indian Philosophies,* 81–83.

31. This, I believe, is also one of the dangers in any uncritical treatment of the *adhyāsa* (superimposition) doctrine, since this may be misconstrued as supportive of subjective idealism. Śaṅkara clearly refutes this idea.

32. BUBh 1.1. 4.

33. We are dealing here also with the all of the negative associations of the word "desire." The perspective of the Bhagavadgītā is helpful and interesting. Kṛṣṇa identifies himself (7:11) with desire that is not contrary to *dharma.* He also (3:25) commends actions of the learned that are motivated by the desire for world wellbeing and offers himself as an example of such action (3:22–24).

34. TUBh 2.6.1, 346.

35. *tasmai sa hovāca prajākāmo vai prajāpatiḥ*

36. BSBh 1.4.14, 271.

37. BSBh 2.1.34, 362–63.

38. BSBh 2.1.35–36, 364–65.

39. See BSBh 2.1.9, 218; BGBh 15:4.

40. While not introduced in the body of this discussion, we must also take note of the tendency to represent *nirguṇa brahman* as impersonal and *saguṇa brahman* as personal and to present the former as higher and superior. This issue is well-discussed in Bradley J. Malkovsky, "The Personhood of Śaṅkara's *Para Brahman.*" His conclusion, with which this study concurs, is that *brahman,* while transcending ordinary human modes of understanding personhood, "is surely not less than personal."

41. See Chapter 1.

CHAPTER 7. LIBERATION

1. T. W. Organ, *The Self in Indian Philosophy* (The Hauge: Mouton & Co., Publishers, 1964), 104.

2. BSBh intro., 3.

3. Organ, *The Self in Indian Philosophy,* 104.

4. BUBh 4.4.6, 502.

5. BSBh 1.1.4, 32.

6. Govind Chandra Pande, *Life and Thought of Śaṅkarācārya,* 226

7. BUBh 4.4.6, 502.

8. For a comprehensive treatment of the idea of *jīvanmukti* in Advaita, see Andrew O. Fort, *Jīvanmukti in Transformation* (Albany: State University of New York Press, 1998).

9. KaUBh 2.2.2, 193.

10. KaUBh 2.3.4, 213. See also Śaṅkara's commentary on Kena Upaniṣad 2.5, and Bṛhadāraṇyaka Upaniṣad 4.4.7.

11. BUBh 4.4.7, 506. Śaṅkara seems to have an appreciation for the human limitations of the liberated person in his claim that, owing to the effects of past actions, memories may "suddenly appear and throw him into the error of regarding them as actual false notions" (BUBh 1.4.10, 116). Constant efforts need to be made, therefore, to "regulate the train of remembrance of the knowledge of the Self by having recourse to means such as renunciation and dispassion" (BUBh 1.4.7, 93). Such momentary lapses do not imply that the fundamental error of taking oneself to be different from *brahman* has not been overcome or that the measures adopted for ensuring the continuity of knowledge are an alternative to the Upaniṣads.

12. My translation.

13. See also 2.5.1.

14. See also 2.7.1.

15. See BUBh 4.4.8, 509.

16. KeUBh 4.9, 96.

17. Madhavananda's translation.

18. For a discussion of the three bodies, see ch.3.

19. See BS 4.2.8. For a more detailed discussion on life after death from an Advaita perspective, see Anantanand Rambachan, "Hinduism," in *Life After Death in World Religions*, ed. Harold Coward (Maryknoll: Orbis Books, 1997), 66–86.

20. "The mind is called the subtle body, Liñga, because it is the principal part of the latter; or the word 'Liñga' may mean a sign, that which indicates the self.—Therefore, only on account of this attachment of his mind, he attains the result through that action. This proves that desire is the root of transmigratory existence." BUBh 4.4.6, 499.

21. See BUBh 4.4.6, 499–500.

22. BUBh 3.2.11, 306.

23. MUBh 2.2.6, 166.

24. See, for example, BSBh 1.2.17, 132, and BGBh 14:3, 380.

25. See BSBh 4.1.13, 837.

26. BSBh 4.1.15, 839. See also MUBh 2.2.8. 138–39, and BGBh 4:37, 150.

27. BSBh 4.1.15, 840.

28. BGBh 2:25, 108. See also BGBh 5:7–8, 163–64.

29. MUBh 1.2.13.

30. The majority of teachers in the Upaniṣads, on the other hand, are not renunciants and they live their lives in family settings. This offers a valuable resource for rethinking the meaning and implications of the liberated life.

31. See AUBh intro., 12, and BRUBh 4.4.6, 500.

32. See BRUBh 4.5.15, 551–52.

33. My translation.

34. BGBh 6:32, 199–200.

35. Fort, *Jīvanmukti in Transformation,* 174. Fort makes a similar argument in "*Jīvanmukti* and Social Service in Advaita and Neo-Vedānta," in *Beyond Orientalism: The Work of Wilhelm Halbfass and Its Impact on Indian and Cross-Cultural Studies,* ed. Eli Franco and Karin Preisendanz (Amsterdam-Atlanta: Rodopi, 1997), 489–504.

36. See above, ch.5.

37. R. Puligandla, *Fundamentals of Indian Philosophy,* 225. See also Swami Prabhavananda, *The Spiritual Heritage of India,* 289–90.

38. See above, ch. 6.

39. See above, ch. 5.

40. Prabhavananda, *The Spiritual Heritage of India,* 289–90.

41. Puligandla, *Fundamentals of Indian Philosophy,* 225. Also Chandradhar Sharma, *A Critical Survey of Indian Philosophy,* 252.

42. Hacker has also established that the radical distinction between a higher (*nirguṇa*) and lower (*saguṇa*) *brahman* will not find much support in Śaṅkara. Śaṅkara also uses terms such as *īśvara, param brahman, nirguṇa brahman,* and *parameśvara* with greater fluidity. See "*Distinctive Features,*" 94–96.

43. See above, ch. 6.

44. See above, ch. 5.

45. BUBh 3.5.1, 333.

46. BSBh 4.4.17, 908–909.

47. For a balanced appraisal of the debate on the composition of the hymns, see G. C. Pande, *Life and Thought of Śaṅkarācārya,* 122–26. Pande is open to the possibility of Śaṅkara as the author of some of these hymns.

48. P. Sankararanarayan, *What Is Advaita?* 57–58.

49. TU, introduction. See also invocations at the begnning of his commentaries on the Māṇḍūkya and Bṛhadāraṇyaka Upaniṣads.

50. *Om saha nāvavatu saha nau bhunaktu saha vīryaṁ karavāvahai tejasvi nāvadhītamastu mā vidviṣāvahai.*

Bibliography

PRIMARY SOURCES IN SANSKRIT

Bhagavadgītā with Śaṅkarabhāṣya. Works of Śaṅkarācārya in Original Sanskrit, Vol II. Pune: Motilal Banarsidass, 1929; reprinted Delhi, 1981.

Brahmasūtra with Śaṅkarabhāṣya. Works of Śaṅkarācārya in Original Sanskrit, Vol III. Delhi: Motial Banarsidass, no date.

Śaṅkara's Upadeśasāhasrī. Ed. Sengaku Mayeda. Tokyo: Hokuseido Press, 1973.

Śvetāśavatara Upaniṣad with Śaṅkarabhāṣya. Pune Ananda Ashram, 1982.

Ten Principal Upaniṣads with Śaṅkarabhāṣya (Īśa, Kena, Kaṭha, Praśna, Muṇḍaka, Māṇḍūkya, Taittirīya, Aitareya, Chāndogya, and Bṛhadāraṇyaka). Works of Śaṅkarācārya in Original Sanskrit, Vol.I. Delhi: Motial Banarsidass 1964, reprinted Delhi, 1981.

PRIMARY SOURCES IN ENGLISH TRANSLATION

*Page references to Śaṇkara's commentaries are from these translations.

* Gambhirananda, Swami, trans. *Eight Upaniṣads with the Commentary of Śaṅkarācārya (Īśa Kena, Kaṭha,* and *Taittirīya* in vol. I; *Aitareya, Muṇḍaka, Māṇḍūkya* and *Kārika,* and *Praśna* in vol. II). 2nd ed. Calcutta: Advaita Ashrama, 1965–1966.

*———, trans. *Brahma-Sūtra-Bhāṣya of Śaṅkarācārya.* 3rd ed. Calcutta: Advaita Ashram, 1977.

*———, trans. *Śvetāśvatara Upaniṣad With the Commentary of Śaṅkarācārya.* Calcutta: Advaita Ashram, 1986.

Jagadananda, Swami, trans. *Upadeśasāhasrī of Śrī Śaṅkarācārya (A Thousand Teachings).* 5th ed. Madras: Sri Ramakrishna Math, 1984.

*Jha, Ganganatha, trans. *The Chāndogyopanishad (A Treatise on the Vedānta Philosophy Translated into English with the Commentary of Śaṅkara).* Pune: Oriental Book Agency, 1942.

———, trans. *The Pūrva Mīmāṁsā Sūtras of Jaimini with an Original Commentary in English.* Varanasi: Bharatiya Publishing House, 1979.

*Madhavananda, Swami, trans. *The Bṛhadāraṇyaka Upaniṣad with the Commentary of Śaṅkarācārya*. 5th ed. Calcutta: Advaita Ashrama, 1975.

———, trans. *The Vedānta Paribhāṣa of Dharmarāja Adhvarīndra.* Belur Math, Howarah: The Ramakrishna Mission Saradapitha, 1972.

———, trans. *Vivekacūdāmaṇi.* Calcutta: Advaita Ashrama, 1978.

Mahadevan, T. M. P., trans. *The Hymns of Śaṇkara.* Delhi: Motilal Banarsidass, 1980.

Mayeda, Sengaku, trans. *A Thousand Teachings: The Upadeśasāhasrī of Śaṅkara.* Albany: State University of New York Press, 1992.

Nathan, R. S., trans. *Tattva Bodha of Śaṅkarācārya.* Calcutta: Chinmaya Mission, no date.

Nikhilananda, Swami, trans. *Vedāntasāra or The Essence of Vedānta of Sadānanda Yogīndra.* 6th ed. Calcutta: Advaita Ashrama, 1974.

———, *Dṛg Dṛśya Viveka.* Mysore: Sri Ramakrishna Ashram, 1970.

Olivelle, Patrick, trans. *The Upaniṣads.* Oxford: Oxford University Press, 1996.

Prasad, R. C., trans. *Śrī Rāmacaritamānasa.* Delhi: Motilal Banarsidass, 1984.

*Sargeant, Winthrop, trans. *The Bhagavad Gītā.* Albany: State University of New York Press, 1984.

*Sastry, A. Mahadeva, trans. *The Bhagavadgītā with the Commentary of Śaṅkarācāraya.* Madras: Samata Books 1977; reprinted 1979.

*Thibaut, Georges, trans. *Vedānta Sūtras with the Commentary of Śaṅkarācārya*, Vols. 34 and 38 of *Sacred Books of the East.* Delhi: Motilal Banarsidass, 1988 and 1981.

SECONDARY SOURCES

Balasubramanian, R., ed. *The Tradition of Advaita.* Delhi: Munshiram Manoharlal, 1994.

———. *Advaita Vedānta.* Madras: University of Madras, 1976.

Bhattacharya, Kalidas. *Recent Indian Philosophy.* Vol.1. Calcutta: Progressive Publishers, 1963.

Cenker, William, *A Tradition of Teachers: Śaṅkara and the Jagadgurus Today.* Delhi: Motilal Banarsidass, 1983.

Chaitanya, Svarupa. *Tattva Bodha of Sankaracharya.* Bombay: Central Chinmaya Mission Trust, 1993.

Chatterji, S. C., and D. M. Datta. *An Introduction to Indian Philosophy.* Calcutta: University of Calcutta, 1960.

Clooney, Francis, X. *Theology After Vedānta: An Experiment in Comparative Philosophy.* Albany: State University of New York Press, 1993.

Comans, Michael. *The Method of Early Advaita Vedānta.* Delhi: Motilal Banarsidass, 2000.

———. "The Question of the Importance of *Samādhi* in Modern and Classical Advaita Vedānta," *Philosophy East and West* 43, no.1 (1993): 19–38.

———. "Śaṅkara and Prasaṅkhyāvāda," *Journal of Indian Philosophy* 24 (1996): 49–71.

Coward, Harold, ed. *Life After Death in World Religions*. Maryknoll: Orbis Books, 1997.

Dasgupta, S. *A History of Indian Philosophy*. 5 Vols. Delhi: Motilal Banarsidass, 1975.

Deutsch, Eliot. *Advaita Vedānta: A Philosophical Reconstruction*. Honolulu: East-West Center Press, 1985.

Deussen, Paul. *System of the Vedānta*. Delhi: Oriental Reprint, 1979.

———. *The Philosophy of the Upanishads*. Delhi: Oriental Reprints, 1979.

Devaraja, N. K. *An Introduction to Śaṅkara's Theory of Knowledge*. Second rev. ed. Delhi: Motilal Banarsidass, 1972.

Fort, Andrew O. *Jīvanmukti in Transformation*. Albany: State University of New York Press, 1998.

———. "Jīvanmukti and Social Service in Advaita and Neo-Vedānta." In Eli Franco and Karin Preisendanz eds., *Beyond Orientalism: The Work of Wilhelm Halbfass and its Impact on Indian and Cross-Cultural Studies*. Amsterdam-Atlanta: Rodopi, 1997, 489–504.

———. *The Self and Its States: A States of Consciousness Doctrine in Advaita Vedānta*. Delhi: Motilal Banarsidass, 1990.

——. "Beyond Pleasure: Śaṅkara on Bliss," *Journal of Indian Philosophy* 16, no. 2 (1988): 177–89.

Gispert-Sauch, G. *Bliss in the Upaniṣads*. Delhi: Oriental Publishers, 1977.

Grant, Sara. *Toward An Alternative Theology*. Notre Dame: University of Notre Dame Press, 2002.

Grimes, John. *Problems and Perspectives in Religious Discourse: Advaita Vedānta Implications*. Albany: State University of New York Press, 1994.

Halbfass, Wilhelm. *Tradition and Reflection: Explorations in Indian Thought*. Albany: State University of New York Press, 1991.

———. *India and Europe*. Albany: State University of New York Press, 1988.

———, ed. *Philology and Confrontation*. Albany: State University of New York Press, 1995,

Hiriyanna, M. *Essentials of Indian Philosophy*. London: Unwin Paperbacks, 1978.

Indich, William, M. *Consciousness in Advaita Vedānta*. Delhi: Motilal Banarsidass, 1980.

Ingalls, D. H. "Śaṅkara on the Question: Whose Is avidyā?" *Philosophy East and West* 3 (1953–54): 69–72.

Isayeva, Natalia. *Shankara and Indian Philosophy*. Albany: State University of New York Press, 1993.

James, William. *The Varieties of Religious Experience*. Glasgow: William Collins, 1979.

Kattackal, Jacob. *Religion and Ethics in Advaita*. Frieburg: Herder, 1980.

Loy, David. "The Religion of the Market," *Journal of the American Academy of Religion* 65/2, 1997.

Mahadevan, T. M. P. *Outlines of Hinduism*. Bombay: Chetana Limited, 1977.

Malkovsky, Bradley J. *The Role of Divine Grace in the Soteriology of Śaṅkarācārya*. Leiden: Brill, 2000.

———. "Advaita Vedānta and Christian Faith," *Journal of Ecumenical Studies* 36, no. 3–4 (Summer–Fall 1999): 397–442.

———. "The Personhood of Śaṅkara's *Para Brahman*," *Journal of Religion* 77 (1997): 541–62.

———, ed. New Perspectives on *Advaita Vedānta*. Leiden: Brill, 2000.

Menon, Keshava, Y. *The Mind of Shankara*. Bombay: Jaico Publishing House, 1976.

Murty, Satchidananda. *Revelation and Reason in Advaita Vedānta*. Delhi: Motilal Banarsidass, 1974.

Nakamura, Hajime. *A History of Early Vedānta Philosophy. Part I.* Delhi: Motilal Banarsidass, 1983.

Nirvedananda, Swami. *Hinduism at a Glance*. Calcutta: Ramakrishna Mission, 1979.

Organ, T. W. *The Self in Indian Philosophy*. The Hague: Mouton, 1964.

Osborne, Arthur. *Ramana Maharshi and the Path of Self-Knowledge*. New York: Samuel Weiser, 1970.

Pande, G. C. *Life and Thought of Śaṅkarācārya*. Delhi: Motilal Banarsidass, 1994.

Potter, Karl, H. *Advaita Vedānta up to Śaṅkara and His Pupils* (Encyclopedia of Indian Philosophies, Vol. III). Delhi: Motilal Banarsidass, 1981.

Prabhavananda, Swami. *The Spiritual Heritage of India*. Hollywood: Vedanta Press, 1979.

Puligandla, R. *That Thou Art : Wisdom of the Upaniṣads*. California: Asian Humanities Press, 2002.

———. *Jñāna-Yoga-The Way of Knowledge*. Lanham: University Press of America, 1985.

———. *Fundamentals of Indian Philosophy*. Nashville: Abingdon Press, 1975.

Radhakrishnan, Sarvepalli. *Indian Philosophy*. 2 Vols. Bombay: Blackie and Son, 1983.

Raju, P. T. *The Structural Depths of Indian Thought*. Albany: State University of New York Press, 1985.

Rambachan, Anantanand, *Accomplishing the Accomplished: The Vedas as a Source of Valid Knowledge in Śaṅkara*. Honolulu: University of Hawaii Press, 1991.

———. *The Limits of Scripture: Vivekanada's Reinterpretation of the Vedas*. Honolulu: University of Hawaii Press, 1994.

Rao, Srinivasa. "Two Myths in Advaita," *Journal of Indian Philosophy*, 24, no. 3 (June 1996): 265–79.

Russell, Peter. *From Science to God.* Novato: New World Library, 2003.

Sankaranarayanan, P. *What is Advaita?* Bombay: Bharatiya Vidya Bhavan, 1988.

Saraswati, Dayananda Swami. *Introduction to Vedānta.* Delhi: Vision Books, 1989.

———. *The Teaching of the Bhagavadgītā*. Rishikesh: Sri Gangadhareswar Trust, 1985.

Satprakashananda, Swami. *The Universe, God, and God-Realization*. St. Louis: The Vedanta Society of St. Louis, 1977.

Sharma, Arvind. *The Experiential Dimension of Advaita Vedānta*. Delhi: Motilal Banarsidass, 1993.

Sharma, Chandradhar. *A Critical Survey of Indian Philosophy*. Delhi: Motilal Banrasidass, 1983.

The Tales and Parables of Sri Ramakrishna. Madras: Sri Ramakrishna Math, 1980.

Smith, Huston. *The World's Religions*. New York: Harper Collins, 1991.

Stephens, Lynn G., and Gregory Pence. *Seven Dilemmas in World Religions*. New York: Paragon House, 1994.

Warrier, A. G. Krishna. *God in Advaita*. Simla: Indian Institute of Advanced Study, 1977.

Whitfield, Carol. "The Jungian Myth and Advaita Vedanta." Unpublished PhD Dissertation. Graduate Theological Union, 1992.

Index